Culture and Customs of Libya

Recent Titles in
Culture and Customs of Africa

Culture and Customs of Libya

TOYIN FALOLA, JASON MORGAN, AND BUKOLA ADEYEMI OYENIYI

Culture and Customs of Africa
Toyin Falola, Series Editor

 GREENWOOD

AN IMPRINT OF ABC-CLIO, LLC
Santa Barbara, California • Denver, Colorado • Oxford, England

Library of Congress Cataloging-in-Publication Data

Falola, Toyin.
    Culture and customs of Libya / Toyin Falola, Jason Morgan, and Bukola Adeyemi Oyeniyi.
        p. cm. — (Culture and customs of Africa)
    Includes bibliographical references and index.
    ISBN 978–0–313–37859–1 (hardcopy : alk. paper) — ISBN 978–0–313–37860–7 (ebook)
1. Libya—Civilization. 2. Libya—Social life and customs. I. Morgan, Jason. II. Oyeniyi, Bukola Adeyemi. III. Title. IV. Series: Culture and customs of Africa.
DT222.F35   2012
961.2—dc23   2012010875

ISBN: 978–0–313–37859–1
EISBN: 978–0–313–37860–7

16 15 14 13 12   1 2 3 4 5

This book is also available on the World Wide Web as an eBook.
Visit www.abc-clio.com for details.

Greenwood
An Imprint of ABC-CLIO, LLC

ABC-CLIO, LLC
130 Cremona Drive, P.O. Box 1911
Santa Barbara, California 93116-1911

This book is printed on acid-free paper ∞

Manufactured in the United States of America

To the people of Libya for a new beginning

Map of Libya. (Cartography by Bookcomp, Inc.)

Contents

CONTENTS

Series Foreword

AFRICA IS A VAST continent, the second largest, after Asia. It is four times the size of the United States, excluding Alaska. It is the cradle of human civilization. A diverse continent, Africa has more than 50 countries with a population of over 700 million people who speak over 1,000 languages. Ecological and cultural factors vary from one region to another. As an old continent, Africa is one of the richest in culture and customs, and its contributions to world civilization are impressive indeed.

Africans regard culture as essential to their lives and future development. Culture embodies their philosophy, worldview, behavior patterns, arts, and institutions. The books in this series intend to capture the comprehensiveness of African culture and customs, dwelling on such important aspects as religion, worldview, literature, media, art, housing, architecture, cuisine, traditional dress, gender, marriage, family, lifestyles, social customs, music, and dance.

The uses and definitions of "culture" vary, reflecting its prestigious association with civilization and social status, its restriction to attitude and behavior, its globalization, and the debates surrounding issues of tradition, modernity, and postmodernity. The participating authors have chosen a comprehensive meaning of culture while not ignoring the alternative uses of the term.

Each volume in the series focuses on a single country, and the format is uniform. The first chapter presents a historical overview, in addition to information on geography, economy, and politics. Each volume then proceeds to

examine the various aspects of culture and customs. The series highlights the
mechanisms for the transmission of tradition and culture across generations:
the significance of orality, traditions, kinship rites, and family property distribu-
tion; the rise of print culture; and the impact of educational institutions. The
series also explores the intersections between local, regional, national, and
global bases for identity and social relations. While the volumes are organized
nationally, they pay attention to ethnicity and language groups, and the links
between Africa and the wider world.

The books in the series capture the elements of continuity and change in
culture and customs. Custom is represented not as static or as a museum arti-
fact but as a dynamic phenomenon. Furthermore, the authors recognize the
current challenges to traditional wisdom, which include gender relations,
the negotiation of local identities in relation to the state, the significance of
struggles for power at national and local levels and their impact on cultural
traditions and community-based forms of authority, and the tensions
between agrarian and industrial/manufacturing/oil-based economic modes
of production.

Africa is a continent that is experiencing great changes, instigated mainly
by Africans but also by influences from other continents. The rise of youth
culture, the penetration of the global media, and the challenges to genera-
tional stability are some of the components of modern changes explored in
the series. The ways in which traditional (non-Western and nonimitative)
African cultural forms continue to survive and thrive—that is, how they
have taken advantage of the market system to enhance their influence and
reproductions—also receive attention.

Through the books in this series, readers can see their own cultures in a different perspective, understand the habits of Africans, and educate themselves
about the customs and cultures of other countries and people. The hope is
that readers will come to respect the cultures of others and see them not
as inferior or superior to theirs but merely as different. Africa has always been
important to Europe and the United States, essentially as a source of labor,
raw materials, and markets. Blacks are in Europe and the Americas as part
of the African diaspora, a migration that took place primarily because of the
slave trade. Recent African migrants increasingly swell their number and visibility. It is important to understand the history of the diaspora and the newer
migrants as well as the roots of the culture and customs of the places from
where they come. It is equally important to understand others in order to

be able to interact successfully in a world that keeps shrinking. The accessible nature of the books in this series will contribute to this understanding and enhance the quality of human interaction in a new millennium.

Toyin Falola
Frances Higginbotham Nalle Centennial Professor in History
The University of Texas at Austin

Preface

THIS BOOK FOCUSES ON the customs and culture of Libya from antiquity to the present. Libya, a relatively new state in North Africa, achieved independent statehood in 1951. It is one of five states in the Maghreb region. Libya derives its name from *Libue*, a name originally used by the Greeks to describe the entire region of Northwest Africa with the exception of Egypt. Archaeological evidence from as early as 8000 BCE, such as rock art, paintings, and engravings, in Wadi Teshuinat, Wadi Mattendush, El Awrer, Wadi Tiksatin, Messak Settafet, and Messak Mellet in southwest Libya and also Jebel Acacus in western Libya reveals that Neolithic peoples inhabited the coastal regions of ancient Libya. These unintended and mute witnesses to events, peoples, and generations past reveal that the Libyan Sahara was once a home to rivers, grassy plateaus, and abundant wildlife, such as giraffes, elephants, and crocodiles. In addition, the archeological record reveals that the Sahara was once a temperate zone, home to lakes and dense forests. Perhaps, drawn by the temperate climate, which played important roles in the growth and development of their customs and cultures, the Neolithic peoples were ardent livestock managers and cultivators of crops.

Libya has a tumultuous ancient and contemporary history. For thousands of years, Libya was conquered, occupied, and administered by outsiders. The Greeks, who founded Cyrenaica in 632 BCE, were the first. The Romans, after destroying Carthage at the end of the Third Punic War in 146 BCE, extended their influence across the region to include Tunisia and, a century later, Tripolitania and the entire area of modern-day Libya. The sentiment behind Emperor Julius Caesar's infamous declaration *Carthago delenda est*[1] failed to prevent the Vandals from overrunning Roman territories, including Libya, in 442 BCE. The Vandals were a Germanic tribes who crossed into North Africa from Spain in 429 BCE.

After the death of Prophet Mohammad in 632 AD, Arab armies initiated a campaign of militarism and proselytism that eventually brought about half of the known world under the Ottomans. The Byzantine provinces of Egypt, Syria, Persia, and North Africa proved more attractive early prizes to the Ottomans and, about 643 AD, the Arabs occupied Alexandria. Cyrenaica followed in 644, Tripolitania in 646, Fezzan in 663, and Tunisia in 670. Thus, by 715, the Arab Empire stretched north to the Pyrenees (in Spain) and to all of North Africa. In the twentieth century, European colonial expansion and imperialistic ambitions led Italy to invade and occupy Libya between 1911 and 1922. The modern name Libya was first used by the Italians in 1934 to describe its North African colonial provinces; much of the area includes present-day Libya. In 1951, Libya became an independent state.

The customs and cultures of these outside influences on Libya were not only different but sometimes ambivalent. Conquered and occupied for much of its history, Libya lost socioeconomic and political control of its land but certainly not its customs and culture, as this book shows. While the Greeks and the Roman invaders were, for the most part, pagans and animists, the Ottomans and the Italians were, and still are, Muslims and Christians, respectively. The Greeks and Romans left indelible marks on Libyan architecture, the Ottomans on religion, and the Italians on culinary culture. However, modern Libyans have adapted and mixed ancient, traditional practices with "imported" ones to reinvent a society that is steeped in sociopolitical and religious traditions that have made Libya not only unique in its political organization but also in its cultural sophistication. By emphasizing the changes Libya has witnessed over the years, this book shows the dynamic nature both of Libyan culture and customs and of the nation's growth and development.

Essentially, this book focuses on contemporary Libya, especially the various events that have shaped the lives of the young nation and its people since independence in 1951 through late 2011. The primary concerns of the authors are twofold: to introduce the customs and culture of Libya to curious readers and to demonstrate that the ongoing political revolution in Libya, as in most of North Africa and the Middle East, is not an isolated development but one with deep historical roots. In other words, *Culture and Customs of Libya* provides not just a window into the past of this North African nation but also a window into its future. It offers a nuanced analysis of current and future socioeconomic and political developments in Libya.

Heuristic studies on Libya are few. This is, in part, because of the repressive nature of the Libyan government under Muammar Qaddafi. Until fairly recently, Libya remained a closed society. Although Qaddafi claimed Libya was a "People's Republic," Libya and Libyans did not enjoy freedom of association, thought, or peaceful assembly. Libyans could not openly criticize their government. The use of English was, until very recently, prohibited, and Libya was, by all estimates, a police state. Despite these sociopolitical repressions, Libya is also a nation with rich traditions, customs, and culture that define its conservative outlook.

The commercial exploration of crude oil soared in the 1970s and accelerated industrialization and urbanization in Libya. Oil wealth and growing cities, coupled with improved educational systems and globalization, most especially the development of information and communication technologies, have introduced unprecedented economic and social change in Libya. However, significant cultural changes have also taken place, especially in urban centers. For example, contemporary Libyan music shares a great deal with music in neighboring Egypt; Egyptian rap and pop music are popular in Libyan cities.

Social customs have also changed. Male and female Libyans mingle freely. Marriage customs and ceremonies as well as sartorial traditions that were traditionally Arabic in form and character are taking on new, more modern expressions. For example, women often wear jeans along with veils, and men are often seen in public wearing tee-shirts and jeans. Forced marriage is no longer tolerated; Libya's government has enacted laws giving women a greater voice on marriage-related issues. Education, especially for girls, has increased throughout Libya during the past fifty years. These cultural and social developments are among many other changes in modern-day Libya.

Thus, from antiquity to colonial occupation to the contemporary period, Libyan customs and culture have changed and developed in a great variety of ways. This book makes a heuristic inquiry into Libyan history and society. Libyans have borne several dramatic changes and developments, especially since the late twentieth century, with great courage and fortitude. The legacy of the recent overthrow of Qaddafi marks a new turning point in a long series of socioeconomic, political, and cultural changes in the many incarnations of this dynamic North African nation. The challenges Libya faces today will lead to nothing short of a complete transformation of the country. For good or ill we cannot know for certain. The task of rebuilding postrevolution and post-Qaddafi Libya is not limited to forming a government that will unite the various groups but also includes rebuilding Libyan institutions. However, as this book demonstrates, Libya is not starting from nothing. It is building on a rich cultural tradition borne of its ancient and contemporary experiences.

This book captures Libya at the end of 2011, a Libya newly emerging from the grasp of its deposed eccentric leader, a time when Libya had been cut off from the West for decades. Because of the nature of Qaddafi's police state, what information we do have is pieced together from many sources; this work is a collection of this data. We are indebted to the various scholars who have struggled to understand the "hermit kingdom," and ordinary Libyans who have kept their culture vibrant and available on different platforms, including the Internet. As usual with works like this, all mistakes are ours.

Toyin Falola, Jason Morgan, and Bukola Oyeniyi

Note

1. *Carthago delenda est* (Latin) is Emperor Julius Caesar's famous declaration on the fate of Carthage, which means "Carthage must be destroyed!" The phrase is also attributed to Cato the Elder.

Chronology

1228–1574	Hafsid Dynasty
1517	Ottomans occupy Cyrenaica
1551	Ottomans occupy Tripoli
1711–1835	Karamanli Dynasty
1803	*Philadelphia* captured off coast of Tripoli
1835	Second Ottoman occupation
1908	Young Turk Revolt
1911–1943	Italian occupation
1912	Congress of Aziziyyah
November 1918	Tripoli Republic created
1929	Cyrenaica, Tripolitania, and Fezzan united as Libya
September 1931	Libyan resistance to Italian occupation ends
1938	Italy creates large agricultural settlements
1943	British and French military administration of Libya begins
February 1947	Italy formally relinquishes control of Libya
November 1949	United Nations General Assembly passes a resolution creating an independent Libya
December 1951	United Kingdom of Libya proclaims independence under King Idris al-Sanusi
February 1953	Libya joins Arab League
October 1961	Libya begins exporting oil
1962	Libya joins OPEC
April 1963	Federal government abandoned in favor of unitary state
September 1969	September Revolution, Colonel Muammar Qaddafi overthrows monarchy
June 1970	Americans evacuate Wheelus Air Force Base
1971	Libya orders foreign military bases closed and nationalizes property of Italian settlers
April 1973	Qaddafi declares a "cultural revolution" based on the Third Universal Theory
August 1973	Libya begins nationalizing oil companies

September 1975	United States issues sanctions on Libya
March 1977	Establishment of the People's Authority
December 1979	U.S. embassy attacked in Tripoli
January 1980	French embassy burned in Tripoli
February 1980	United States closes its embassy in Tripoli
March 1980	Private savings accounts are outlawed
1980s	Qaddafi supports terrorist groups, including the Irish Republican Army (IRA) and various radical Palestinian factions.
1986	Libya found responsible for a bomb blast at a Berlin discotheque frequented by U.S. troops.
May 1981	United States orders Libyan embassy in United States closed
August 1984	Libya and Morocco sign Treaty of Oujada
April 1986	Benghazi and Tripoli struck by U.S. airstrikes; U.S. fighter jets bomb Libya, killing 101 people, including Qaddafi's adopted daughter
August 1986	Morocco withdraws from Union with Libya
1988	Suspected Libyan agents bomb Pan Am Flight 103 over the Scottish town of Lockerbie, killing 270 people, mostly Americans
February 1989	Algeria, Libya, Mauritania, Morocco, and Tunisia create the Arab Maghreb Union
August 1991	Libya opens Great Manmade River
April 1992	United Nations imposes sanctions on Libya
November 1992	Libya demands compensation for Italian occupation
November 1994	Libya revalues its currency
September 1995	Government forces clash with Islamists in Benghazi
April 1996	Qaddafi stops all business with Western companies
March 1997	Vatican establishes diplomatic relations with Libya
October 1998	South Africa grants Qaddafi the Order of Good Hope for his support of the anti-apartheid movement
April 1999	UN sanctions are suspended

1999	Qaddafi hands over two Libyans charged in the Lockerbie bombing
March 2000 municipal	Libya dissolves most of executive branch and grants power to councils
September 2000	Racial violence breaks out throughout the nation
2001	A Scottish court acquits one of the Lockerbie bombers and convicts Abdelbaset al-Megrahi, sentencing him to life imprisonment
October 2001	Libya gains seat on the UN Social and Economic Council
2002	U.S.-Libya talks aim to mend relations, but the United States adds Libya to the "axis of evil" list
2003	Libya acknowledges responsibility for the Lockerbie bombing, agrees to pay up to $10 million to the relatives of the 270 victims, and declares it is dismantling all its weapons of mass destruction
September 2003	All remaining UN sanctions are lifted
December 2003	Libya stops its production of unconventional weapons
June 2004	United States and Libya restore diplomatic relations
September 2004	United States removes trade embargo against Libya
October 2004	European Union lifts arms embargo
May 2006	Libya removed from U.S. list of state sponsors of terrorism
July 2006	Libya classified as one of the least-diversified economies in OPEC by the World Bank
2009	Libya holds celebrations marking Qaddafi's 40 years in power; al-Megrahi is released from a Scottish prison on compassionate grounds because he has prostate cancer
February 16, 2011	Riot police clash with protesters in Benghazi, Libya's second-largest city; protesters burn security headquarters and police stations in two other cities; Qaddafi responds by doubling salaries of government employees and releasing 110 suspected Islamic militants
February 17, 2011	Protesters defy police crackdown and take to the streets in 5 cities; at least 20 are killed in clashes with progovernment groups

February 20, 2011   Anti-Qaddafi protests spread to Tripoli, the capital; more
                           than 200 people killed in 5 days; Qaddafi's son, Seif
                           al-Islam, proclaims on state television that his father
                           remains in charge with the army's backing and will "fight
                           until the last man, the last woman, the last bullet"

February 21, 2011   Anti-Qaddafi protesters claim control of Benghazi;
                           Libyan diplomats abroad and the justice minister at
                           home resign; air force pilots defect as fire burns the main
                           government hall in Tripoli; New York–based Human
                           Rights Watch puts the overall death toll of the conflict
                           at 233

August 21, 2011   Anti-Qaddafi protesters claim control of Tripoli; Qaddafi's
                           palatial home overrun by protesters

1

Introduction

ALTHOUGH THE COUNTRY NAMED LIBYA is relatively new, the name Libya has been around for a long time. Ancient Egyptians used Libya to describe the desert people living beyond their western frontier. The early Greeks used it for all non-Punic Africans living west of the Egyptian borders, while the Romans used it for all Africans living on Carthaginian territory. However, the name was not used to describe the people and land officially known today as Great Socialist People's Libyan Arab Jamahiriya until the early twentieth century. Its modern usage began in 1911 when Italy invaded the provinces earlier held by the Ottomans. Italy used the name in its attempts to justify its aggression by linking the area to the former North African territories of the Roman Empire. After 1929, the name Libya came into use when the Italians formally joined and administered Tripolitania, Cyrenaica, and Fezzan under one governor.

Since achieving independence in 1951, Libya has changed its name four times. It was named the United Kingdom of Libya at independence. In 1963, its name changed to the Kingdom of Libya, and in 1969, it was the Libyan Arab Republic. It was known as the Socialist People's Libyan Arab Jamahiriya in 1977, and, later in the same year, its name was further changed to Great Socialist People's Libyan Arab Jamahiriya. In spite of all these changes, the general name remained Libya, and it is by that general name that the country will be referred to.

Sand dunes stretch into the distance on the northern edge of the Sahara desert at al-Ramla in western Libya. (AP Photo/John Moore)

Geographically, Libya is bordered on the north by the Mediterranean Sea, on the east by Egypt, while Sudan lays to the southeast. Chad and Niger lay to the south and Algeria and Tunisia to the west. Although Libya is a relatively large country in terms of land mass—slightly larger than the state of Alaska—its population is a little above six million. Though separated from the rest of Africa by the immense Sahara desert, Libya is linked to the fate of the continent. However, it is culturally, linguistically, and religiously linked with the Arab population of the Middle East and prides itself as an Arab nation. For millennia, Libya has relied on both the vibrant trans-Saharan trade routes and its key ports along the Mediterranean. Along with the other nations of North Africa, Libya has consistently linked sub-Saharan Africa with the trading networks of both Europe and Asia, and, because of this, it has an identity that is Arab, Mediterranean, and African.

Libya has been conquered, settled, occupied, and ruled by various Mediterranean powers; hence, its indigenous arts, architecture, culture, and people bear the imprints of these various nations. Since the eighth century BCE when the Phoenicians settled in Libya, Libya has been a key player in the Mediterranean. Carthage, Greece, Rome, the Arabs, the Ottoman Empire, and Italy all, at one point or another, ruled over Libya. These Mediterranean powers, however, were able to rule only the coastal areas of contemporary Libya, as the vast Sahara Desert prevented them from conquering or effectively ruling the Berber population who lived and controlled the desert. All of the colonial powers associated with Libya relied on the native Berber population to make the great trek across the Sahara and return to the Mediterranean with the riches of sub-Saharan Africa.

LAND

With a land area totaling 679,358 square miles (1,759,540 square kilometers) and a population estimate of 6,461,454 as of 2010, Libya is a small country. It is straddled between Tunisia and Algeria along the northeastern coast and to the south by Sudan, Chad, and Niger. Arable plateau land suitable for agriculture is available along the Mediterranean coast and farther inland, but much of the country lies within the Sahara desert and is dry.

Although Libya is generally low lying with two northern upland areas, about 93 percent of its land area is semidesert. To the south of Libya, the land rises to form the *Tibesti* and *Uweinat* Mountains. In addition to water courses known as *wadis*, which flow during the rainy seasons, a great reservoir of water is underground. Other than these courses, the country lacks any permanent flowing rivers.

CLIMATE AND TOPOGRAPHY

Libya has two climatic zones: the Mediterranean climate, which is limited to the coastal areas in the northern portion of the country, and the tropical climate of the southern regions. The Mediterranean is characterized by warm dry summers, cold winters, and precipitation of up to 24 inches (600 mm), which is limited to between October and March. The tropical climate of the south is characteristically hot and dry, with occasional rainfall that seldom exceeds 19 inches (500 mm) annually. The country's wind system is usually from the north and east between May and October, and north and west between November and April. Temperatures differ across the regions. In Tripoli, temperatures range from between 46 and 61 degrees Fahrenheit (8 and 16 degrees Celsius) in January, while in August it reaches as high as between 72 and 86 degrees Fahrenheit (22 and 30 degrees Celsius).

Approximately 93 percent of Libya's land area is either semidesert or in the heart of the Sahara desert. The harsh climate compels many Libyans to reside around the Mediterranean coast. The principal topographical regions are Western Muqataa or Tripolitania, Eastern Muqataa or Cyrenaica, and

Southern Muqataa or Fezzan. Tripolitania and Cyrenaica are situated on the Mediterranean coast and are more Mediterranean in their religious affiliation, identity, and culture. Fezzan, on the other hand, is located in the Sahara and is more African in its cultural identity.

ECONOMY

With about 1.8 million square kilometers of land area, Libya is the fourth largest country in Africa and the seventeenth largest country in the world. Owing largely to its oil and gas reserves and a relatively small population, Libya's Human Development Index is the highest in Africa. Its gross domestic product (GDP) per capita is also the fourth highest in Africa behind Seychelles, Equatorial Guinea, and Gabon. Globally, Libya's oil and gas reserves are rated as the tenth largest proven oil and gas reserves, and the country is also the seventeenth highest petroleum-producing nation globally.

Revenue from the oil and gas sector is the mainstay of the Libyan economy. With a GDP that stood at US$32.9 billion in 1994, the sector constitutes practically all of Libya's export earnings. Since 1959, when oil and gas were discovered in commercial quantities in Libya, the sector has provided about one-quarter of Libya's GDP. Oil and gas transformed Libya from a poor economy to one of the richest economies in Africa. In the early 1980s, Libya was among the wealthiest countries in the world, with a higher GDP per capita than Italy, Singapore, South Korea, Spain, New Zealand, and some other developed economies. However, with oil exports worth an estimated US$37 billion a year, contemporary Libya has been described by the World Bank as the least diversified member of the Organization of Petroleum Exporting Countries (OPEC).

Boasting one of Africa's highest GDPs per capita, Libya was able to provide extensive social security for its citizens, especially in housing and education. Notwithstanding its small population and high revenues from oil and gas, the Libyan unemployment rate stands at 21 percent according to 2010 census figures—the highest in all of North Africa.

Bolstered by a huge financial outlay from the oil and gas sector, Libya has carried out enormous economic reforms aimed at reintegrating the country into the global capitalist economy since September 2003 when the United Nations (UN) and the United States lifted sanctions. These reforms included joining international organizations, especially the World Trade Organization; reducing government subsidies for products and services; and privatizing government institutions. These reforms revamped Libya's economy and helped it develop modern cities that rival those in the west.

Other sectors have also been expanded. For example, Libya's construction sector now accounts for about 20 percent of the country's GDP. The agricultural

Tripoli residents take a bath in drinking water that finally reached the Libyan capital in August 1996. (AP Photo/Lino Azzopardi)

sector has evolved from processing mostly agricultural products to producing petrochemicals such as fertilizer. Other agricultural products include barley, citrus fruits, dates, groundnuts, livestock, olives, tobacco, and wheat. Libya's major industries, including oil and gas production or refining, food processing, agriculture, cement production, fishing, textiles, and handicrafts, continue to provide opportunities for trading partners (e.g., Italy, Germany, France, Spain, and Turkey) and ample economic opportunities for individuals in the private sector.

However, problems in Libya persist. Despite huge earnings from oil and gas, Libya's public debt stood at US$2.592 billion in 1992. Although authorities have privatized more than a hundred government-owned companies (most especially in oil refining, tourism, and real estate) since 2003, its imports and exports stood at US$4.386 billion and US$7.826 billion, respectively. Despite climate and poor soils that severely limit agricultural output, Libya imports nearly 75 percent of its food. Access to drinking water has improved, yet more than 28 percent of the population still lacks access to safe drinking water. It is important to note that since 2003, considerable efforts have been made to tap into vast underground fresh water aquifers. The aquifers were discovered while searching for oil around the Great Manmade River. When completed, it is hoped the Great Manmade River will also improve the country's agricultural output.

Contemporary Libya's economy is best described as a blend of capitalism and socialism. During the 1970s, the government nationalized a number of important industries and redistributed wealth among the population. Although in the 1990s the Libyan government implemented policies it believed would diversify the economy and lead to a more market-based system, Libya's key industries are presently owned by the government.

GOVERNMENT

Libya, having been mandated by the UN General Assembly to become independent before January 1, 1952, declared its independence on December 24, 1951. Its name at independence was the United Kingdom of Libya. The country was a constitutional and hereditary monarchy under King Idris, Libya's only monarch. In 1951, the Libyan National Assembly drafted and enacted the Libyan Constitution; the *Official Gazette*, the official publication of the national government, published the constitution in the same year.

One of the major concerns at the United Nations before 1951 was how an independent Libya would coordinate and unite its three different regions—Tripolitania, Fezzan, and Cyrenaica—into a single Libyan state. Hence, the immediate concern of the new government under King Idris was the formulation of a Libyan government and the enactment of a constitution that placed a high premium on fundamental human rights common to nations in much of Europe and North America. However, Article 5 of the constitution, which proclaimed Islam as the religion of the State, runs counter to Article 11 of the constitution, which sets out basic rights such as equality before the law, equal civil and political rights, equal opportunities and responsibility "without distinction of religion, belief, race, language, wealth, kinship or political or social opinions."

After 1959, oil wealth made it possible for King Idris to achieve economic prosperity. Libya, a country the United Nations originally feared would be among the poorest nations of the world, emerged as an extremely wealthy state. Although oil exploration improved Libya's economy at this early stage, it created resentment that led to the rise of Nasserism and Arab nationalism among some factions. These factions regarded concentration of all power over the nation's wealth under the control of the monarch as detrimental to their existence. The increasing number of Americans, Italians, and British that were granted contracts and employed in extensive engineering projects in Libya added to the discontent Libyans felt with King Idris. In addition to engineering and construction contracts, the United States and Britain supplied almost all of Libya's arms. Moreover, the United States' Wheelus Air

Base, which was set up to monitor the former Soviet Union's influences around North Africa, was established in Libya during this period.

In the late 1960s, at the height of this discontent, a small group of military officers led by Muammar Qaddafi, a 27-year-old army officer, staged a coup d'état that removed King Idris from power and launched the Libyan Revolution on September 1, 1969. In 1973, Qaddafi delivered a nationwide address called the "Five-Point Address," in which he launched an administrative and cultural revolution aimed at purging those he described as being "politically sick." He announced the implementation of Sharia and the suspension of all existing laws. Under Qaddafi, Libya's government, supposedly a *Jamahiriya* (Arabic for "ruled by the masses"), was in reality an authoritarian state.

Qaddafi set out the essence of the new Libyan government in *The Green Book*. This publication was to evolve into a balance between Capitalism and Marxism that he called the Third Universal Theory. The theory demanded dismantling all existing governmental and social structures and establishing a "direct democracy" where citizens govern through grassroots activism and without any intervention whatsoever from state institutions or from the military, clans, *ulama*, or academic intelligentsia. In 1977, as part of the processes for implementing this direct democracy, Qaddafi dismantled all state structures and declared Libya a "state of the masses."

Although he claimed to have dismantled all structures of government, he mainly instituted new structures, particularly after 1987. Under Qaddafi's new system, the primary instrument of government was the General People's Congress (GPC), which was both an executive and legislative body. The GPC replaced the Revolutionary Command Council (RCC), which was comprised exclusively of soldiers who carried out the coup that removed King Idris from power. Unlike the RCC, the GPC met three times a year. Although members of the former RCC primarily composed the newly constituted GPC, a small General Secretariat headed the GPC. Below the GPC was the General People's Committee, which replaced the erstwhile Council of Ministers. Like the former Council of Ministers, the new General People's Committee functioned as a cabinet. Next to the General People's Committee, the People's Committee allowed for subnational representation and participation. The committees were organized into wards at the urban level, villages at the rural level, and at municipal levels. Other structures of government under Qaddafi included the Basic Popular Congress (BPC) and Arab Socialist Union (ASU), which was the only legally recognized political organization.

Until recently, contemporary Libya had two branches of government: the revolutionary and Jamahiriya sectors. The revolutionary sector was headed by the Revolutionary Committee, a 12-person committee headed by

The leaders of Egypt, Libya and Syria sign a treaty of confederation in Benghazi, Libya, on April 17, 1971, joining their countries into the Union of Arab Republics. Seated at left is Egyptian President Anwar Sadat; seated in the center is Libyan head of state Colonel Muammar Qaddafi; Syrian President Hafez Assad is on the right. (AP Photo)

Qaddafi, the Revolutionary Leader. The Revolutionary Committee members were the same members of the former 12-person Revolutionary Command Council established in 1969 at the beginning of the Revolution. Members of the revolutionary sector were not elected. They were all appointed by Qaddafi; therefore, the people could not vote them out of office. They owed their right to power to their involvements in the planning and execution of the coup that led to the revolution; until recently, they headed the government.

The Jamahiriya sector was comprised of representatives elected by the people from each of the 1,500 urban wards for the Basic People's Congresses and 32 elected representatives from the various regions for both the Sha'biyat People's Congress and the National General People's Congress. Constitutionally, these were legislative bodies. These congresses were, in turn, represented by corresponding executive bodies, the Local People's Committees, Sha'biyat People's Committees, and the National General People's Committee or Cabinet, respectively. Elections were held every four years to choose members of the Basic People's Congresses and to choose secretaries for the People's Committees. Leaders of the Local People's Congress represent their

A caricature of Libyan dictator Muammar Qaddafi being crushed by the rebel pre-Qaddafi flag is seen on a wall in rebel-held Benghazi. (AP Photo/Sergey Ponomarev)

communities' local congress at the People's Congress, while members of the National General People's Congress elect representatives to the National General People's Committee (the Cabinet) during annual meetings. Although Qaddafi desired to replace subnational and traditional leadership with corps of administrators who possessed the capacity to modernize Libya, in practice, the system of government he introduced disfranchised Libyans and turned Qaddafi into a dictator.

PEOPLE

According to 2010 census estimates, Libya's population rose from its 2006 estimate of 5,670,688 million to 6,420,000 million. About 89 percent of the population is of mixed Arab-Berber background. Other ethnic minorities include Berbers, Tuaregs, Harratins, and Black Africans or Tebous. Thousands of immigrants from Egypt, Italy, Greece, Croatia, Malta, Tunisia, and Armenia also make Libya their home. Libya's dominant ethnic group is the Arabs. The Arabs, who arrived in North Africa by the beginning of the seventh century, established an Arabic system of government, Islam, and the Arabic language in Libya. By 1300, the indigenous Berber, Tebou, and Tuareg populations had been converted to Islam, and the Arabic language replaced the indigenous Berber dialects. The Arabs live primarily in the coastal regions of Tripolitania and Cyrenaica.

The second largest ethnic group in Libya is the Berbers. They were a part of the formerly dominant ethnic group in North Africa. To escape invasion and successive waves of Arab migration, the Berbers lived principally in remote areas, primarily in the mountainous or desert locales. In the 1980s, 135,000 people, constituting about 5 percent of Libya's total population, were either Berbers or native speakers of Berber dialects.

In the southwest desert, about 10,000 Tuaregs are nomads, living in scattered communities and wandering in the general vicinity of the oasis towns of Ghat and Ghadamis. These Tuaregs claim close relationships with other, much larger Tuaregs population in Algeria and elsewhere in the Sahara. The Tuaregs, like other desert nomads, earn their livelihood by engaging in long-distance trading, extracting protection fees from travelers and caravans, and raiding neighboring sedentary settlements. In southern Libya, about 2,600 Tebou live near the well-populated borders of northern Chad, Niger, and Sudan.

LANGUAGES

Libyans generally consider themselves Arabs. Arabic, a Semitic language, is the mother tongue of most people in North Africa and the Middle East. Arabic is the official language of Libya, though a small minority of Libyans speaks other languages. However, in Fezzan, especially the southern regions, some remnants of the Berber languages are still spoken. In the southwestern deserts, the Tuareg language Tamasheq, a Berber dialect, is widely spoken. In the southernmost part of Libya, Tebou is spoken among the small group of indigenous people of the same name. English and Italian are also understood in the major cities.

Since the One September Revolution, Qaddafi tried to prevent Libyans from speaking any language except Arabic. He banned English language classes and books written in English in Libyan schools. His attempts to unify the nation under a common language also led him to limit foreign language programs in Libyan schools and cultural centers.

HISTORY

Ancient History

As early as 8000 BCE, ancient Libya was inhabited by Neolithic people. Perhaps these people migrated into the area as they foraged for roots and fruits, and hunted game; they may also have been lured by the climate to settle in the area. The lush green vegetation, temperate climate, and arable land enabled the Neolithic culture to grow. Rock art and paintings, carvings, and other archaeological remains, largely in present-day Southern Libya's Wadi Mathendous and Jebel Acacus, reveal that prehistoric Libya had developed a pastoralist culture, as today's Libyan Sahara was then covered with rivers and grassy plateaus that were rich in wildlife such as giraffes, elephants, and crocodiles. Ancient Libyans were comprised essentially of Berbers, Tuaregs, and Black Africans. They were skilled in not only animal husbandry, most notably cattle, but also in cultivating crops.

Climatic change led to rapid desertification, which compelled some of these ancient people to disperse to other places such as the Siwa Oasis in Egypt. Garamantes, undoubtedly the indigenous Libyan civilization based in Germa, probably reached its zenith at this time, when the Sahara was yet still green. The Garamantes were an aboriginal Saharan people, predominantly of Berber origin, who were distinguished for their use of elaborate underground irrigation channels they used to water their fields. They founded their kingdom in the Fezzan area, where they existed as a tribal people by 1000 BCE They were undoubtedly a local power remarkable for their livestock production and farming in the Sahara between 500 BCE and 500 CE. The Lebu, Berbers, Garamantes, and other ethnic groups living in the Sahara were already well established at the time the Phoenicians, the first Semitic people, arrived in Libya from the East.

Phoenicians and Greeks in Libya

The first Mediterranean people to establish any contact with ancient Libyans were merchants from Tyre, in modern-day Lebanon. As early as the first millennium, these merchants developed commercial relations and made treaties with the Berber ethnic groups in Libya to ensure their cooperation in the exploration and exploitation of Libya's raw materials. By the fifth century BCE, Carthage, arguably the greatest of the Phoenician colonies, extended its socioeconomic and political domination across much of North Africa, giving birth to the remarkable Punic civilization. The earliest centers of Punic civilization in Libya were the coastal cities of Oea (present-day Tripoli), Libdah (present-day Leptis Magna), and Sabratha. These coastal cities were in various stages of social and political development when the Phoenicians arrived. The areas were ruled as a single entity and collectively called Tripolis, which means the Three Cities. The current capital of modern Libya is derived from the name.

The Pentapolis, or the Five Cities, were Barce, presently known as Al Marj; Euhesperides, later called Berenice and presently known as Benghazi; Taucheira, later called Arsinoe and presently known as Tukrah; and

The ruins of the Agora, which was once a public square, forum, and market in the ancient Greek city of Cyrene in northeast Libya. (AP Photo/Nasser Nasser)

Apollonia, later called Susah. The Five Cities were established at the port of Cyrene. Cyrene grew to become one of the greatest intellectual and artistic centers of the Greek world, most remarkable for its medical school, its learned academies, and its superlative architecture. Together with Cyrene, these five cities became known as Cyrenaica.

The Greek colonies in Libya were perpetually under intense challenges from the neighboring frontiers: by the Egyptians from the East and by the Carthaginians from the West. The Greeks held their ground in Libya until 525 BCE, when Persian armies under Cambyses II overran Cyrenaica. The Persians ruled Libya for two centuries. Alexander the Great of Macedonia would eventually replace Cyrus the Great of Persia when he defeated the Persian Empire in 331 BCE.

The Phoenician city-state of Carthage emerged as a powerful trading empire in the Western Mediterranean by the third century BCE, and its empire stretched from Libya across North Africa to modern-day Spain. The growth of Carthaginian power happened simultaneously with another emerging Mediterranean power: Rome. However, between 264 and 146 BCE, Rome and Carthage fought a series of wars, the Punic Wars, to decide who would control the Mediterranean world. Rome emerged victorious, and Carthage was sacked in 146 BCE Rome appropriated all territories controlled by

Carthage, including Tripolitania and Cyrenaica, in 74 BCE Carthage became a Roman supply post and a center of trade for consumer goods such as ivory, ostrich feathers, and salt.

Roman Libya

Rome controlled the western part of Libya until around 44 BCE, when Julius Caesar undertook a land grant policy to compensate Roman soldiers who served him in his campaigns. These Roman soldiers turned to farming and moved to North Africa to cultivate their holdings. Libya, under Roman control, invariably became the bread basket of Rome. Although Rome conquered Carthage in 74 BCE, it did not take possession until a century later. When it did, its rule remained limited to the region around Tripoli. However, under Julius Caesar, Roman armies began to move east towards Benghazi, and they slowly conquered Egypt. Leptis Magna, which today boasts some of the most complete ruins of a typical Roman city, was the most important Roman city in Libya.

Leptis Magna owed its immense wealth to its location. The city was situated on a protected bay and experienced abundant rainfall that made it suitable for cultivation. The city also benefited from the fact that two Roman emperors, Septimius Severus (who ruled from 193 to 211 CE) and his son Caracalla (who ruled from 211 to 217 CE), were born in Leptis Magna and claimed it as their hometown. Both Septimius and Caracalla invested heavily in their hometown of Leptis Magna. They built, among other things, amazing structures for the arts and everyday infrastructure like aqueducts and baths. However, by the fourth century, Leptis Magna was abandoned as the harbor became filled with silt, and the Berbers made the security situation in Leptis Magna untenable.

Roman North Africa suffered from a number of revolts and Berber raids in the third century. The revolts were fuelled by excessive Roman taxation. Non-Romans were taxed and persecuted throughout North Africa, which led to an increase in tensions until Rome eventually granted its Libyan provinces autonomy in 305. In addition to the revolts, raids, and loss of a major city, the growth of Christianity in the region also weakened Roman rule. Many Berbers converted to Christianity. For the Africans, accepting Christianity was an act of protest against Rome; hence, they embraced Christianity with reckless abandon. North Africa, including Libya, became one of the leading centers of early Christianity. Before Emperor Constantine made Christianity an accepted religion in the early fourth century, it had already been accepted by the Roman authorities in North Africa.

Roman rule in North Africa lasted until the early fifth century when Germanic groups from Eastern Europe invaded the entire Roman Empire.

One of these groups, the Vandals, fought all the way to Spain and then crossed over to North Africa, destroying everything in their path. By the middle of the fifth century, the Vandals had conquered North Africa, including Tripolitania, and they ruled the Western portion of North Africa for a century. The Vandals's rule in Tripolitania ended in 534, when Emperor Justinian from Byzantium, a Roman city-state in the East, reconquered the region.

Byzantine rule in the region failed to achieve the level of development the earlier Roman Empire attained. In fact, the Byzantines were able to hold on to only the coastal cities. Byzantine rule in Tripolitania was defensive in nature; the indigenous population would raid and attack any Romans who ventured outside the city walls. The weakness of the Byzantine Empire in North Africa made the region ripe for conquest by the rising power of the Arabs in the seventh and eighth centuries.

Arab Invasions

A decade after the death of Prophet Muhammad, Arab armies led a campaign of proselytism, which led to the religious conversion and conquest of half of the known world. Byzantine provinces of Syria, Egypt, and Persia were early targets; however, Alexandria was not occupied until 643, followed by Cyrenaica in 644, Tripolitania in 646, Fezzan in 663, and Tunisia in 670. By 715, the Arab armies stopped at the Pyrenees, the mountains separating Spain from France.

Although Libya had been subjected to invasion and occupation by outsiders throughout its history, it was the Arab invasion in the seventh century that had the most long-term impact, especially in terms of language and religion. When Arab armies took Tripolitania in 646, they used it as a base to further their attacks on Byzantine possessions in North Africa. The Arabs succeeded in conquering and defeating the Byzantine forces along the coast of Libya and other parts of North Africa, but they were unable to control the interior. Like the Byzantine armies a century earlier, the Arab armies were not able to completely destroy the Berbers. However, over the course of a few decades, many Berbers in Libya converted to Islam and voluntarily joined the Arab armies. In 682, the Arab armies reached the Atlantic coast.

As earlier noted, language and religion were the two fundamental areas where Arabs had the greatest impact on Libya. Today, most Libyans consider themselves Arabs and Muslims. It must be noted, however, that it was not the Arab invaders who spread Islam throughout the region, but the Berbers who adapted Islam to their beliefs and carried the religion far into the interior of the Sahara and beyond. Orthodox Islam and the Arab population mostly stayed in the coastal cities of Libya and tried to rule with a soft hand in the rural areas.

Arab rule in North Africa was technically a theocracy, although a caliphate headed the region and acted as both king and religious leader. In principle, the caliph exercised complete control over his subjects, but in reality, Arab rule was one of negotiation. In the urban areas, Islamic and Arab soldiers dominated the political and religious scene; in the countryside, the Berbers refused to bow down to Arab dominance. The Berbers preferred to continue raiding and warring against the new Arab possessions; they were not subdued until the eleventh century when the Caliphate invited a number of Bedouin groups from Saudi Arabia to help crush the Berber rebellion.

Thousands of Bedouins answered the call, and the nomadic warriors swept through Egypt into Libya. Major cities of Libya were destroyed, and those coastal Berbers who were not annihilated were assimilated into Bedouin culture. Over the next several hundred years, Libya became a battleground for Arab and Berber populations, until both were defeated by a resurgent Christian Spain in the sixteenth century. Spanish armies conquered Tripolitania but were unable to hold it when another Muslim power moved in. By the end of the sixteenth century, Tripolitania was ruled by the Ottoman Empire.

Ottoman Rule

The Ottoman Empire, which began in Anatolia (Turkey) near the present-day city of Istanbul around the fourteenth century, conquered Constantinople, the Byzantine capital, and pushed into central Europe by the mid-1500s. Between 1529 and 1683, the Ottomans attempted to take the capital of the Hapsburg Empire Vienna twice and were defeated both times. They did, however, maintain possession of southeast Europe until the nineteenth century. As they expanded into Europe, the Ottomans also conquered the Middle East and a significant portion of North Africa, which the Ottomans controlled into the twentieth century. From the sixteenth and seventeenth centuries, the Ottomans and Hapsburgs, whose empire stretched from Spain to modern Germany, struggled to control the Mediterranean.

Ottoman rule in Libya lasted until the Italian conquest in 1911. Like the Arabs and the Byzantine Empire that preceded them, the Ottomans were able to control only the coastal cities, never Libya's interior. Libya's fertile plains, from which the Romans derived enormous wealth, had been destroyed by centuries of warfare and were of little economic value to the Ottomans, with the exception of their strong ports and strategic location, which enhanced the Ottoman's efforts to control the Mediterranean.

Until 1711, Ottoman Libya was used primarily as a base for piracy against Hapsburg ships. Throughout the eighteenth and nineteenth centuries, neither the Hapsburgs nor the Ottomans were able to overpower the other, but the Ottomans used Libya to their advantage as a base for hijacking Hapsburg ships. Piracy in this period was predicated on capturing foreign vessels and then demanding enormous ransom for the vessels, crews, and cargoes. Piracy of this sort became the main source of income for Libya during the first part of Ottoman rule.

Within Libya, incessant coups and revolutions disrupted Ottoman rule. At its very height, the Ottomans requested that Turkey send the Janissaries, the backbone of the Ottoman army. The Janissaries were originally Christian slaves derived primarily from the Balkans who were trained as soldiers. Originally, the Janissaries were an elite military force, loyal only to the Ottoman emperor. However, as they were dispatched further away from the Ottoman metrople, they often became mercenaries, fighting for the highest bidder in colonial wars.

In 1611, local chiefs staged a coup and forced the sultan to appoint one of them as pasha (governor). Over the next few decades, the power of the pasha declined as Janissaries gained greater control. Between 1672 and 1711, the Janissaries fought among themselves, and local rulers rarely controlled their territory for more than a year before they were removed by the military. Tripoli especially saw coup after coup, while the Ottomans looked the other way for as long as the region remained profitable and revenues poured into their coffers.

Karamanli Dynasty

In 1711, Ahmed Bey Karamanli, a *khouloughli* cavalry officer, overthrew the pasha of Tripoli, seized power, and founded a dynasty that governed Tripoli for the next 124 years. Recognizing the Ottoman suzerainty, Karamanli created a quasi-independent, dynastic military garrison composed of a largely Arab government. He bought the title of Pasha-Regent from the Ottoman sultan with money taken from his coup against Turkish officials, and he ruled Tripoli until his death in 1745. The Karamanli dynasty under Ahmed operated its own foreign policy with Europe that primarily focused on trade. Ahmed brought great wealth to Libya not only from privateering but also from tapping into the trans-Saharan trade. After conquering Cyrenaica, the Karamanli dynasty controlled two of the most important outlets for the trans-Saharan trade in the Mediterranean. Ahmed also sent punitive expeditions into the Sahara and subdued the Berbers enough that his heirs incorporated Fezzan under their rule. Ahmed Bey Karamanli created a relatively strong Libya that was virtually autonomous, and he created a stable and prosperous society.

However, shortly after his death, things in the country unraveled, as Ahmed's heirs lacked the administrative or military skills of their forbearer. Throughout the mid-eighteenth century, the wealth and power left by

Ahmed declined. A series of droughts and famine further crippled the economy under Ali, Ahmed's grandson, in the 1790s. The collapse of the Karamanli dynasty allowed a minor Turkish official to overthrow Ali and briefly return Ottoman rule to the region in 1793. But the Turkish official was deposed two years later by Yusuf, Ali's son. Yusuf looked to his great-grandfather's legacy for guidance and, once again, began to break away from Ottoman control and exercise his own foreign policy. He invaded Fezzan and subdued the Berbers. He also supported Napoleon Bonaparte's invasion of Egypt against the wishes of both the Ottoman and British governments. Yusuf allowed Napoleon to use Tripoli as a base for his Egyptian campaign.

Yusuf recognized the importance of the trans-Saharan trade and revived the trade. He also created a modern navy to protect Libya's interests. As his navy grew, Yusuf began to demand that European powers recognize Libyan control of the central Mediterranean and pay fees for safe passage. Libyan privateers set upon the ships of those nations that refused to pay. Piracy proved extremely profitable for Yusuf. However, by 1815 when the Napoleonic Wars ended, the European powers refused to pay for protection, and piracy quickly declined in the region. Yusuf increasingly relied on taxation and borrowing money, which led to discontent among his subjects and, in 1831, Fezzan revolted. The revolt spread throughout Libya, and the rebels forced Yusuf to abdicate for his son Ali II in 1832. Ali II recognized that he could not put down the revolt himself and asked for Ottoman assistance. When the Ottoman fleet arrived, it arrested Ali II and the Ottoman Empire reasserted its control of Libya.

Barbary Pirates and the United States

During the eighteenth and nineteenth centuries, the coast of North Africa, including Libya, was collectively referred to as the Barbary Coast. Privateers operating out of the area were often called Barbary Pirates. These "pirate" principalities included Tripoli, Algiers, Morocco, and Tunis. All operated on the same principle: nations could pay for safe passage of ships, or they could risk attacks by Barbary corsairs who would force them to pay ransom for the return of their ships. When ransoms were not paid, crews were either forced into working for the pirates or sometimes sold into slavery. While the United States was still a British colony, colonial U.S. ships were protected under agreements between the Barbary pirates and the British government. However, once the United States declared independence, American shipping was no longer protected. Throughout the 1790s and into the early 1800s, American ships in the Mediterranean were attacked and captured by the Barbary pirates.

In 1785, the regency of Algiers seized two U.S. ships off their coast, and after trying to negotiate with the French for intervention in 1786, the United

States had its first formal diplomatic exchange with an African state. Thomas Jefferson and John Adams met with the Tripolitanian ambassador in London and tried to negotiate safe passage for American ships. These negotiations failed because the Americans would not pay the fee that the Tripolitanians demanded. Eventually, the United States negotiated the release of its ships and promises of safe passage from the Algerians in exchange for a one-time cash payment and naval supplies. The Algerians negotiated on behalf of Tripoli. In the midst of negotiations, a misunderstanding emerged between the United States and Tripoli; the Algerians had led the Americans to believe that Tripoli was under its control when in fact Tripoli was under the rule of Yusuf Karamanli and, therefore, practically independent.

Yusuf needed funds to fill his treasury and, unencumbered by any direct negotiations with the Americans, began attacking American ships again in 1801, which quickly led to a conflict between the two nations. The United States had recently built up its oceangoing navy and the new president, Thomas Jefferson, wanted to make an example out of Tripoli. Therefore, in 1801, he sent the U.S. Navy into war against the Tripolitanians. Three ships arrived off the coast of Tripoli and immediately blockaded the port. The blockade was relatively ineffective because the Tripolitanians seized the American frigate *Philadelphia* and captured its entire crew. The crew of the other U.S. ship, the *Intrepid*, did not want one of the most powerful ships in the U.S. Navy to be captured and used as a pirate vessel, and it blew up the *Philadelphia* in Tripoli's harbor.

In 1805, the former U.S. consul to Tripoli signed an agreement with Yusuf's brother Ahmed, which would place him in power. Under the command of the consul, a contingent of U.S. marines landed in Cyrenaica, captured the seaport of Darnah, and marched toward Tripoli. As they approached Tripoli, Yusuf made diplomatic moves to avoid a direct conflict, and he signed a peace treaty with the United States. The centerpiece of the treaty included a prisoner exchange and a one-time payment of US$60,000 to Tripoli. The treaty also guaranteed that any future prisoners taken from either of the two nations would be treated as prisoners of war, not as slaves or pirates. The treaty was unpopular in the United States, as some Americans believed Jefferson should have installed Ahmed on the throne as a pro-American power in the region. During both the war and negotiations, the United States dealt solely with Tripoli; the Ottomans stayed out of the war and negotiations.

Repeated economic crises, growing social unrest, and deepening political rivalry characterized the final days of the Karamanli dynasty. After the European powers united to put an end the corsair system, the Libyan economy deteriorated. Yusuf Pasha mortgaged the royal agricultural estate, devalued the local currency as he struggled to pay his mounting debts, and expanded the Saharan slave trade. However, all these efforts could not solve his problems. His efforts to increase customs duties and to impose new taxes on the masses led to civil war.

The Second Ottoman Rule

The Ottomans feared that the development of Egypt under Muhammad Ali might spread to Libya, a development that could possibly transfer control of Libya to Italy. Egypt had never kept its intention to invade Italy a secret. The Ottomans took over Libya in 1835 and ruled it until 1911. In the over 100 years that the Karamanli dynasty ruled Libya, the Ottoman Empire had gone through a major transition in the way that it ruled its empire. It recognized that one of the central problems of the late eighteenth and early nineteenth centuries was that its rule was not centralized enough. In granting regional autonomy, the Ottomans encouraged rebellions in Libya and Egypt. Both North African nations threatened the stability of the region, and Mohammad Ali almost achieved complete independence for Egypt.

Once the Ottomans reestablished their control from Ali II, they unified the region into one *vilayet* (province) under a *wali* (governor-general) who was based out of Tripoli. The Ottoman administrators were all Turks; not a single Arab participated in government. In addition to the *vialye* and *wali*, there were four other subregional provinces beneath the central administration. Because of the civil wars and famines that plagued the end of the Karamanli dynasty, the Ottomans quickly took control of the coastal areas and subdued the restless Berbers further inland. Eventually Cyrenaica got its own *wali* who answered directly to the Ottoman sultan.

By the mid-1850s, the Ottomans instituted a number of reforms in their administration of Libya. These reforms encouraged urbanization, administrative reorganization, commercial development, land reform, and educational development. Institutional reforms included policies that allowed for the creation of administrative and village councils, the establishment and administration of civil and criminal courts, and the introduction of new methods of tax assessment and collection. Infrastructure developments were also made; telegraph lines and other necessary infrastructure were established. The results of these political, institutional, and infrastructural developments were far-reaching and multidimensional. However, of even greater significance was the transformation from pastoralism to sedentary agricultural practices.

Despite improvements, the Ottoman administration in Libya suffered from a few major drawbacks. Administrators and governors were replaced fairly regularly, and the Ottoman Empire was also slowly collapsing.

Concerned with the growing power of Italy, France, and Britain in the Mediterranean and of the Austrians and Russians in the Balkans, the Ottomans fell further and further behind the European powers. In Africa, the British, French, and Italians began to push the Ottomans out, while the Ottomans slowly relinquished territories in the Balkans and Caucasus to the encroaching Russians and Austrians. The last half of the nineteenth century was one of slow decline for the Ottoman Empire before it finally disintegrated following World War I.

Italian Invasion and Occupation of Libya

Italy did not achieve national unity until 1860 and, as a result, it missed out on the imperial land grab of the European powers in the nineteenth century. During the latter part of the eighteenth century, however, Italy eyed the Ottoman colony of Libya. In the early 1900s, Italy viewed itself as the rebirth of the Roman Empire, one that would dominate the Mediterranean and take back some of its lost territories. However, nations much stronger than Italy controlled most of the territory in the Mediterranean. As a result, Italy was forced to look for a weaker opponent, which it found in the Ottoman Empire whose power and importance was already in rapid decline.

To achieve its objectives, Italy declared war on the Ottoman Empire in 1911. More than 30,000 Italian troops seized Tripoli in October 1911. The smaller Ottoman forces retreated into the desert as coastal city after coastal city fell to the Italians. Ottoman military units joined forces with Bedouins and Berbers, and the alliance began to wage a holy war against the Italian invaders. However, threats to the Balkans, an area much more important to the Ottomans, forced the sultan to negotiate a truce with the Italians. In October 1912, the sultan decreed that Tripolitania and Cyrenaica were independent, and Italy immediately announced its annexation of Libya. For the next two decades, the Italian army waged a genocidal war against the Libyans, who viewed the Italian conquest not only as an imposition of foreign rule but also as a war against an infidel army.

By 1913, opposition under the Sanusiya Order, a religious movement in Cyrenaica, and organized forces in Tripolitania and French forces in Fezzan forced the Italians to reconsider their position in Libya. The Italian army concentrated on the coastal regions and, by the outbreak of World War I, pushed many of the Libyan opposition forces away from the coastal regions. Once World War I began, Italy was forced to withdraw some of its forces from Libya to fight in Europe, a move that allowed the Libyan forces to operate more freely.

By the middle of World War I, Sanusiyan forces, under the leadership of Ahmad ash-Sharif, forced the Italians out of Cyrenaica. The Ottoman

Empire joined World War I on the side opposing Italy and Great Britain, and it convinced Sharif that he should invade British Egypt under the guidance of Turkish officers. Sharif's forces were quickly destroyed by the British, and he was forced to step down in favor of Idris. Both Italy and Britain recognized Idris as the Amir of Cyrenaica. After World War I, the victorious powers recognized Italy's control of Libya against the objections of Idris and other Libyan nationalists. In 1918, Tripolitania tried to arrange the same structure of loose control that Cyrenaica practiced under Idris, but it was unable to find a person that it could rally behind. The Italians flirted with controlling Libya through a system of indirect rule, but Benito Mussolini came to power in Italy. Mussolini, enchanted by stories of Libya's fertile lands and believing that Italy should play a major role in global politics, wanted firm control of Libya.

In 1923, the Italian army once again invaded Cyrenaica and drove the Sanusiyan forces into the desert. The army was able to take Benghazi, most of Tripolitania, and Fezzan, but the Sanusiyans would not go down quietly. Idris fled for his life, but Sheik Omar Mukhtar waged a guerilla war against the Italians that lasted until 1931. Although Mukhtar was outgunned and outmanned, he nevertheless waged a valiant struggle for the independence of Cyrenaica. Over half a million Libyans were believed to have died during the eight-year war against Mukhtar as the Italians sought to consolidate their hold on Libya. The Italians utilized concentration camps, slash-and-burn policies, and other genocidal acts to discourage bases of support for Mukhtar. Mukhtar was eventually captured and executed, but he remains a hero to the Libyan people for his war against Italian imperialism.

After the defeat of Mukhtar, Mussolini appointed Italo Balbo as the governor of Libya. Balbo believed in the Italian colonization project and actively encouraged Italian settlers to migrate to Libya. By 1940, over 100,000 Italians lived in Libya. Italians received the best land and housing in the cities and coastal plains while native Libyans were treated as servants and second-class citizens. Under Balbo, the Italian government instituted massive modernization projects related to roads, railway lines, hospitals, buildings, schools, and other social amenities that made the Italians feel more at home in Libya. Italian became the official language and was taught in schools, but there was little effort to incorporate the Arab or Berber populations into the colony.

None of the modern amenities established in Libya by the Italians were designed or built for the local Libyan population, and resentment against Italian rule grew among the Libyans throughout the 1930s and into the 1940s.

World War II

During World War II, Italians and Germans fought the British and Americans for control of North Africa; and by 1940 when the Italians invaded British-controlled Egypt, Libya became a battleground. The Italians immediately attacked Egypt, and the Sanusis in Cyrenaica declared their support for the allies; Tripolitania followed shortly afterward. The British army in Egypt quickly pushed the Italians back and, in February 1941, Hitler sent in the famed Afrika Korps under General Erwin Rommel to aid Libya. Rommel, often outmanned and outgunned, spent the next two and a half years chasing the British out of Libya and almost out of Egypt.

During the early stages of World War I, eastern Libya, in particular, was a fierce battleground as the British army and Rommel tried to outmaneuver each other. Benghazi and Tobruk traded hands multiple times as the ebb and flow of war favored each side. Thousands of Libyans joined the British army in a continuation of their long history of opposition to Italian occupation. World War II devastated the countryside of Libya. Tens of thousands of mines littered the country. However, Libya emerged from World War II with hope for the future. When the Sanusis joined the allied cause, the British government promised the Libyans they would never again be ruled by Italy.

Post–World War II Libya

Immediately after World War II, the newly formed United Nations stripped Italy of its colonial possessions, just as the League of Nations took away Germany's territories following World War I. From 1945 to 1951, the status of Libya in the international community remained undetermined. Britain and France wanted to split Libya between the two of them, with Tripolitania joining Tunisia as a French colony and Cyrenaica joining Egypt under British control. The United States had no strong opinion on Libya as long as the Soviets did not get a piece. Joseph Stalin, acting on one of Russia's long-held ambitions, wanted Libya split into occupation zones much like Germany so that the Soviets could gain a port on the Mediterranean.

The United Nations originally kept Libya as an Italian colony administered by British and French governments as it figured out what to do with the country. In 1949, however, the United Nations declared that Libya would become an independent nation by 1952 at the latest and all three of its historic regions would be joined in the new country.

However, for the country to be successful, it had to be economically viable. The ravages of World War II and Italian rule had destroyed Libya's economy. In the end, the people of Libya decided that they could and would work together to form a viable and independent nation. The constitution of the newly formed United Kingdom of Libya granted each of the provinces eight representatives in the national parliament. Equal representation rather than proportional representation based on population allowed the new government to gain the support of the less populous regions of Fezzan and

Cyrenaica not only to enact the national constitution but also to reap dividends when Libya became a sovereign nation in 1951.

Realizing the strategic importance of Libya, both the British and U.S. governments negotiated deals with the Libyan provincial government that allowed each of them to keep military bases in Libya. Using the Wheelus Airfield as its base, the United States agreed to pay $1 million a year to Libya while the British maintained control of its own bases. In a time of rising Arab nationalism in Libya and throughout the Arab world, these bases would cause tension between Libya and the West in the years to come.

United Kingdom of Libya

Libya emerged in 1951 as an independent nation under a constitutional monarchy with King Idris, formerly the Amir of Cyrenaica, as the first and, as future events would reveal, the only king. After the first elections in a free Libya, King Idris and the ruling party disbanded and outlawed all opposition parties in the country, and, within the authority of the constitution, he appointed half of the senators. The constitution also empowered him to veto any legislation of which he disapproved. Idris inherited an impoverished nation: Libya's chief economic activity was selling scrap metals from the battlefields of World War II. Libya also relied heavily on the revenues generated from leasing bases to the United States and Great Britain and on the millions of dollars in aid that arrived for the West every year. Idris's government was effectively pro-Western, mostly out of necessity.

Without Western aid, Libya would have collapsed economically. This state of affairs changed dramatically in 1959 when commercial quantities of crude oil were discovered. Almost overnight, Libya went from being an impoverished nation completely dependent on foreign investment to an extremely wealthy nation. The Libyan government taxed oil revenues at a rate of almost 50 percent, and it granted companies around the world permission to drill in the country. As the oil wealth accrued in government coffers, Idris launched a five-year plan designed to modernize Libya's infrastructure. However, the federalist form of government established in 1951 proved too cumbersome for his ambitions, and Idris ordered that the constitution be amended.

The new constitution created a strong, central monarchy and dissolved regional governments in Cyrenaica, Tripolitania, and Fezzan. The new central government was, indeed, more efficient. However, it created a situation whereby Idris and his government became less and less in touch with the people. Libya's new wealth did not trickle down to the masses as expected. More and more Libyans flocked to the cities where education was available for the first time. This proved to be a double-edged sword: as more and more Libyans became educated, they began to demand more from the government.

King Idris sits at the opening of Libya's first parliament in Benghazi, March 25, 1952. (AP Photo)

The situation was exacerbated by Radio Cairo, which constantly criticized Idris's government for its pro-Western stance. Unanswered demands and public criticism led many Libyans resented Idris's government. The Arab-Israeli War of 1967, a war in which Idris stayed neutral, made matters worse as anti-Western and anti-Israel riots broke out in Benghazi and Tripoli. Idris recognized the danger, changed his stance, and moved further into the Arab camp. His fate was sealed, however, as discontent had been allowed to brew for too long.

One September Revolution

A group of young army officers led by 27-year-old Captain Muammar Abu Minyar al-Qaddafi, called the Free Officers Movement, seized control of the Libyan government on September 1, 1969. King Idris was in Greece for medical care, and the coup d'état was relatively bloodless. The Free Officers Movement created a 12-member Revolutionary Command Council (RCC) to oversee the government. The international community was stunned by the coup, but, after reassurances by Qaddafi and the RCC that all international agreements would be honored and that the revolution was homegrown, international recognition of the government followed relatively quickly. The primary fear was that Idris and his heirs would try to overthrow the government, but Idris quickly squashed those rumors and lived the remainder of his life in exile in Egypt.

After assuming command of the government, the RCC announced the creation of the Libyan Arab Republic. The Libyan Arab Republic embraced anti-imperialist and socialist principles, and its leaders stressed that it would be a government that would not pander to the West but embrace Arab socialism. The RCC promised equality before the law, social justice, freedom, and unity for all Libyans. The younger generation of Libyans, who felt disappointed by Idris's government, overwhelmingly supported the principles of the RCC and hoped for positive changes in Libya. The RCC also announced the creation of a cabinet that would oversee the operation of the government in accordance with the wishes of the RCC, which left little doubt about Qaddafi's control of the country. Qaddafi was promoted to colonel and given command of the armed forces. Thus, he became the new head of state in Libya.

Muammar Abu Minyar al-Qaddafi

When Muammar Abu Minya al-Qaddafi seized power in Libya in 1969, few had any idea who he was. The One September Revolution took the entire world by surprise. Qaddafi was born during World War II to an Arabized Berber family. He was the only surviving son and spent his childhood tending to his father's flocks of goats in the desert. His early education came from religious teachers within his community, and his formal schooling did not begin until he was 11 or 12 years of age. Qaddafi's childhood instilled in him a love of the desert and a deep commitment to Berber family principles, primarily a strong belief in honor, family, and a strict set of moral codes. A life of hard work and simplicity was superior to the corrupting influence of city life. Qaddafi idolized Nasser, the revolutionary president of Egypt, and embraced Nasser's pan-Arabic, anti-imperialist, egalitarian, and socialist teachings. Qaddafi was expelled from his secondary school in 1961 for his involvement in unauthorized political demonstrations. Even at a young age, it appears Qaddafi wanted to transform Libya into the Egypt of Nasser's dreams.

He joined the Libyan military against the objections of his family, who wanted him to stay with them. The military offered Qaddafi not only a chance for socioeconomic advancement but also a place of power within Libya. He was aware that Nasser's revolution in Egypt originated in the military, and the military could be part of any revolutionary change in Libya, the military was the most likely place to be. While in the army, in the mid-1960s, Qaddafi created the Free Unionist Officers movement. He recruited like-minded individuals into his inner circle. By 1969, Qaddafi created a movement powerful enough to take control of the country and secure his rule. Qaddafi's rule lasted for over 40 years.

Libyan leader Colonel Muammar
Qaddafi in Libya, September
1979. (AP Photo)

Revolutionary Libya

Upon seizing power, Qaddafi started implementing his revolutionary
ideals to transform Libya into a strong Arab socialist state. He pressured both
the American and British militaries to remove their bases from Libyan soil
before their leases expired in 1970. By 1970, both countries had removed
their bases. He also confiscated Italian property; nationalized hospitals,
banks, and insurance companies; and dismissed all officers above the rank
of major in the military while simultaneously doubling the size of the military. He removed high-ranking government officials and closed down private
markets in an attempt to destroy what he saw as the exploitative nature of
capitalism.

In the realm of government, he tried to implement people's councils at the
local level to replace the previous government's bureaucracy. However, by
1973, Qaddafi was disappointed in the revolutionary spirit of the Libyan
people who, he believed, were ambivalent about most of his changes. While
his people's councils were popular, he did not believe they went far enough.
Qaddafi challenged the people of Libya to question traditional authority
and to replace all of the old laws in the country with Sharia law. The
revolutionary spirit of Libyans may not have been as much the problem as

the difficult adjustment to rapid change. The rapid changes in Libyan society led to problems because the people's councils were not able to govern as effectively as the career bureaucrats. In 1975, two members of the RCC attempted a coup. Qaddafi responded by purging the government of anyone he felt was disloyal to him and replacing them with his supporters. The abortive coup led to a consolidation of power in Libya under Qaddafi.

In 1976, Qaddafi retreated into the desert to gather his thoughts and upon his return, he published a series of three essays that were collected into a book, *The Green Book*. *The Green Book* was Qaddafi's vision of how the government should be run and the role that religion should play in Libya. The two most important aspects of his philosophy centered on the idea of *Jamahiriya* and the role of imams, or Muslim prayer leaders.

Under the *Jamahiriya*, Qaddafi argued that government should be run by the masses. In itself, *Jamahiriya* implies statelessness, a form of government where the people govern directly without interference from any central government or its agencies and institutions. While this may have been Qaddafi's plan, in practice, the government he established interfered in almost every aspect of people's lives. Regarding religion, Qaddafi argued that a person's relationship with God is personal and as such people do not need religious leaders to tell them what to believe. This angered the established religious leaders in Libya, who rightly felt that such teachings undermined their authority.

Throughout the 1970s, Qaddafi vehemently opponent both Israel and imperialism. He refused to support Israel and supported terrorism, including Palestinian terrorist organizations and groups such as the Irish Republican Army (IRA). Qaddafi viewed the nation of Israel as an expression of Jewish imperialism against the Arabs, and he funneled weapons and money into groups fighting Israel. He also became an active supporter of African liberation movements. Qaddafi supplied arms and training to Africans, particularly groups in Southern Africa fighting against apartheid and colonialism. Qaddafi's support for international terrorism isolated him from the international community and, in 1986, Ronald Reagan ordered the bombings of military installations throughout Libya in response to an attack supported by the Libyan government on a nightclub in Europe.

Throughout the 1980s, Libya became an international pariah. Early in the 1980s, the United States imposed sanctions on Libya. The United States also forbade American companies from doing business with Libya and American citizens from traveling to Libya. In 1988, Pan Am Flight 103 blew up over Lockerbie, Scotland. Two hundred and seventy people were killed in the blast, and, after years of investigation, indictments were filed against two Libyans, both with strong ties to the government. Qaddafi refused to hand over the suspects, and the United Nations placed stringent sanctions on Libya. Throughout the 1990s, these sanctions destroyed Libya's economy and, in a reconciliatory move, Qaddafi extradited the suspects in 1999. One of the two men, Abdelbaset Mohmed Ali al-Megrahi, was convicted in January 2001 of the bombings and sentenced to life in prison. In August 2009, authorities released him on compassionate grounds after a doctor determined that he had only three months to live. Megrahi was welcomed back to Libya as a hero.

By the late 1990s, Qaddafi withdrew his support for international terrorism in an attempt to have sanctions against his country lifted. After Qaddafi turned over the Lockerbie bomber, the United Nations lifted its sanctions, and the United States did same in 2001. After the September 11, 2001, attack on the United States, Qaddafi became a strong supporter of the War on Terror, and Libya slowly redeemed itself from its past actions. Some criticized Qaddafi for supporting the War on Terror while refusing to crack down on dissident groups within Libya.

Libya once again became a prosperous nation, exporting its oil throughout the world. However, mass protests against Qaddafi's government erupted in February 2011. The protests that began in Benghazi shocked the world. By the end of February, the protests spread westward towards Tripoli. Qaddafi's domination of Libyan political and cultural life collapsed after

Anti-Qaddafi Fighters attending the funeral of one of their fallen comrades. (AP Photo/Rodrigo Abd, File)

41 years of control. Unlike previous efforts to remove Qaddafi from power, the changes Libya has undergone recently will completely transform the country; whether this change will be for good or ill remains to be seen. Even if Qaddafi had not been killed, the history of Libya would not have remained the same. The task of rebuilding post-revolution Libya and the challenge of uniting the different ethnic groups in post-Qaddafi Libya will certainly be the main priorities of the new government.

2

Religions and Worldview

RELIGION

RELIGION, AS UNDERSTOOD IN ITS MODERN SENSE, is a collection of creeds, doctrines, belief systems, and worldviews that establish relationships between humans, the universe, and God. Religion has an established place in Libya. Long before the introduction of world religions, people understood the conception of God or the place of God in the universe. When Christianity and Islam became widespread, religion was constructed on bodies of doctrines, creeds, and belief systems. Unlike in Western tradition where religion is an independent belief system and an organizational structure, old Libya's traditional religion was bound up in the people's general way of life: in the economy, politics, culture, and the like. Today, the most popular religion in Libya is Islam.

The term "traditional religion" is a bit misleading, as it generally suggests an unchanging, static phenomenon embedded in the past. In addition, the term suggests a uniformity of beliefs among Libyan communities. The use of "traditional" here simply delineates between three periods: before contact with the many outside groups that invaded and ruled Libya; the period of these invaders' rule; and the period of independence in Libya. The precontact period is described here as traditional Libya. Even with this clarification, it must be stressed that the term "tradition" must not be construed as implying a period in the past where everything was fixed and static. Traditional

Libyan rebels praying. (AP Photo/Alexandre Meneghini)

societies were not static; rather they responded to external and internal stimuli, most especially in cultural practices, customs, religious practices, language, and beliefs.

Libyans, like other Africans before contacts either with Islam or Christianity, believed in one creator who is regarded as the maker of the universe. This Supreme Being was believed to have withdrawn and distanced himself far away from earthly concerns after creating and setting the world in motion. Consequently, Africans organized cults around secondary divinities who were believed to be messengers or go-betweens constantly serving the Supreme Being. Unlike the Phoenicians, Greeks, and Romans, who were animists, ancient Africans believed in a Supreme Being who was distant from mortal humans and could be approached only through secondary divinities.

However, across Africa, this religious belief was not necessarily coded in written bodies of doctrines. There was little need for proselytism because individuals not only knew the importance of religious worship but also respected and considered religious worship as vital for perpetuating their respective families, communities, towns, and villages. In this respect, individuals, families, communities, villages, and towns had their respective deities through whom they offered worship, sacrifices, devotion, and services to the one god. They did not allow diversity of deities to cloud the fact that the only entity to be worshipped was god.

The Africa religious cosmos was characterized by the unity of diverse deities in the overall service to one god, and it permeated different ethnic groups throughout the continent. In spite of many shared beliefs, certain features exist in different parts of Africa that enable us to differentiate religious practices in the East and West from those in the North and South. Distinctive geographical conditions and long histories of trade and cultural contacts within, among, and between these regions account for these features. In West Africa, most especially along the coast, tropical forests boast extravagant vegetation and dense human populations. Unlike West Africa, where agricultural communities supported urban-based civilizations and flourishing markets in produce, for hundreds of years North African cities were oftentimes smaller and confined to the Mediterranean coast, due to the harsh deserts inland. In East Africa where temperate grasslands spread forth, lending themselves to cattle herding and a large pastoralist culture at the base of snowcapped mountains, religious worship and devotion were organized around the worship of the sky and its associated divinities as well as around ancestral spirits. In West Africa, as we have also found in Egypt, especially along the Nile Delta, kings and heads of ethnic groups are associated with divinities and deities. Even land fertility and peoples' welfare are associated with these gods and goddesses.

The Phoenicians, like the Greeks and Romans, were animists who practiced a religion centered on the fertility god, Baal. Baal worship involved sodomy, bestiality, and ceremonial prostitution, among others. The Phoenicians therefore left little or no imprint on Libyan traditional religious beliefs. The religions of both the Romans and Greeks were different only by degrees from those of the ancient Libyans.

Islam

About 97 percent of Libya's total population is Sunni Muslim, and Islam is the official religion of Libya. Islam, which means "submission to God," permeates all aspects of secular and nonsecular life. The Prophet Muhammad established Islam as a monotheistic religion. The Quran, the holy book of Islam, was compiled after Muhammad. Muslims, however, believed that the Quran was revealed to Muhammad by Allah Himself. Muhammad was said to have retired into the mountains to meditate and, under the guidance of Archangel Gabriel, was asked to write down the word of Allah. Because he could neither read nor write, he memorized these words and recounted them to his followers who copiously wrote them down and compiled the scripts later into the Holy Quran. The principal holy books of Islam are the Quran and the Hadith, a book detailing the life and deeds of Prophet Muhammad. These books set out how Muslim societies are to be run and how individual Muslims should live their lives.

Muslims regard Muhammad as the last and, therefore, the final prophet of God in a long line of prophets and messengers. The prophets and messengers include Abraham, Moses, and Jesus Christ. Islam technically shares the teachings of the Bible except that Muslims contest the position that Jesus Christ is the son of God, a foundational belief in Christianity. Muhammad established that God neither begat nor was He begotten and, thereby, demoted Jesus Christ to the realm of a mere messenger. Although Islam rejects Christianity's deification of Jesus Christ, it does share with Christianity concepts such as resurrection of the human soul, the Day of Judgment, the eternal life of the soul, and guardian angels.

The Quran sets out the basic tenets of Islam, just as the Bible sets out those of Christianity. In both religions, utter submission to God remains the most important tenet, except that in Christianity Jesus Christ is regarded as the only way to God. In addition to total submission to Allah, Muslims are required to observe what are called the Five Pillars of Islam. These include the confession of faith (*shahadah*), daily prayer (*salat*), almsgiving (*zakat*), fasting (*sawm*), and pilgrimage to Mecca (*hajj*). Muslims are to pray at five specified times during the day facing Mecca. In most cases, men pray as a group at the mosque under the direction of a prayer leader (an *imam*). Although Islam allows men and women to attend public worship at the mosque, women are nevertheless separated from the men. For the most part, women's attendance in mosques and at other public events is discouraged, and women typically pray and worship in the seclusion of their homes.

Ottoman rule in Libya was most significant in fostering the development and spread of Islam in Libya. Around 610 CE, Prophet Muhammad received divine messages from Allah and began to preach. He denounced the polytheistic paganism that was prevalent in and around Mecca at that time. However, he and his followers fled to Medina because of intense persecution. At Medina, he continued to preach Allah's message, and, after he defeated his detractors in battle, he returned to Mecca triumphantly before his death in 632. He assumed the temporal and spiritual leadership of the community of faithful, mostly Arab followers.

Through *jihads*, or struggles, Islam developed from a small religious community of Arab faithful into a dynamic military and political community under Prophet Muhammad's authority. After Muhammad's death, his followers carried on successfully and, by the seventh century, Islam reached Libya. After a century-long resistance, Muslims defeated the indigenous Berbers. Although Muslims defeated the Berbers, they were limited to the coastal areas and were unable to take their religion into the deserts where many of the Berbers lived. Hence, in Ottoman Libya, Islam was confined to the urban centers. The conversion of the Berbers was delayed until the eleventh century, when widespread conversion of the nomads began.

Pre-Islamic religious traditions in Libya filtered into the formal practices of Islam. Hence, it is common in Libya to find Quranic rituals and principles coexisting with vestiges of traditional African religious beliefs, such as rites to ensure good fortune and good spirits (*jinns*), evil eye, and cult worship of local saints. While this religious syncretism was prevalent in the deserts, city and town dwellers along the coasts developed a more austere orthodox Islam.

As noted in the introductory chapter, Article 5 of Libya's constitution proclaimed Islam as the official religion of the state. Although the constitution established Libya as an Islamic state, the constitution and the government that King Idris led recognized equal civil and political rights, equality before the law, equal opportunities and equal responsibility to the state without any distinctions to religion, beliefs, race, language, wealth, kinship, and political or social opinions (as laid out in Article 11). Upon independence, many Libyans were not committed fully to Islam. However, they retained Islamic habits and attitudes while still recognizing the separation or distinction between religion and the state. When Qaddafi deposed King in 1969, the new leader strived earnestly to reiterate Islamic values, reinforce Libyas' Islamic culture, elevate the status of Quranic law, and, to a large extent, emphasize Quranic practice in everyday lives of Libyans. Today, as was mentioned earlier, almost all Libyans are Sunni Muslims. Adherents of the Sunni type of Islam believe that religion offers both a spiritual direction for individuals and a basis for government policy; hence, it stresses an agreement between religion and the state.

Although almost all Muslims in Libya are Sunni, other major groups include the Shi'a and Sufi. Technically, Sunni and Shi'a are alike in doctrine; small but significant differences between the two sects revolve around the issue of succession to Prophet Muhammad, who died without any male successor. After Muhammad's death, the question of who would succeed the political and religious leader polarized his followers. The Shi'a argued that Muhammad's successor should come from his family, and they appointed his son-in-law Ali as successor. The Sunni, on the other hand, argued that Muhammad's successor should come from within Muhammad's trained inner circle and need not necessarily be a blood relation. Ali was later killed by Sunni followers.

Sufism entails austere, rational, and intellectual qualities, as well as a more expressive, mystical, and personal means of serving God. Sufism is not peculiar to Libya but abounds in many areas of the Muslim world. Sufism aims to create a personal practice of the divine via mystical and ascetic discipline. Its

Qaddafi in 2007. (AP Photo/
Nasser Nasser)

enthusiasts assemble into brotherhoods, and Sufi worship became extremely
widespread in the rural areas of Libya.

During the eighteenth and nineteenth centuries, Sufi groups exercised
great power and played vital roles in the religious renewal that swept across
North Africa. For instance, when the Ottomans could not effectively resist
the encroachment of Christian missionaries in Libya, the Sanusis led revivalist movements that checked the advances of the Christians and carried Islam
into the deserts and other parts of North Africa.

Libya, and it operates under the authority of Islamic law, or Sharia. The
constitution of Libya established the state as Islamic, but it was not until
the 1970s that Qaddafi overturned colonial laws inherited by his regime
and implemented Sharia. Sharia regulates not just religious issues but also
civil and criminal issues. It places restrictions on diet, dress, relationships,
religious worship, and criminal procedures. The *ulama*, a body of Islamic
scholars, is the primary interpreter of Sharia.

Under Qaddafi, the power of the *ulama* waned considerably after he
imposed his own interpretation of Islam and, as an absolute ruler, his views
became the state's views. Qaddafi argued that the Quran was the only

important work in Islam because it was the word of Allah, and the Hadith was written by men and was, therefore, flawed. Qaddafi also argued that since the Quran was written in Arabic, which is the official language of Libya, everyone should be able to read it. He advocated that the people did not need *ulamas* to interpret the Quran. Qaddafi's brand of Islam that he imposed on Libyans was heavily infused with Sufism as practiced by the Sanusi Order, a powerful mystic sect based in Cyrenaica.

Sanusi Order

The Sanusi Order is an Islamic sect that blends orthodox Islamic teachings with Sufism. During the early 1840s, the Order was influential in Tripolitania and Fezzan, but its influence was stronger in Cyrenaica than in any other parts of Libya. Algerian Sayyid Muhammad Bin Ali al-Sanusi, known as the Grand Sanusi, founded the Order. The Order was a religious revivalist movement adapted to desert life that targeted converts among the Bedouins of Cyrenaica.

In the nineteenth century, the Grand Sanusi studied Islam in some of the best Islamic schools in North Africa. He became interested in a more mystical dimension of Islam called Sufism, and he borrowed what he considered useful from Sufism and adapted it into his order. Sufism seeks to set its adherents on a path to get closer to Allah; hence, the Sufis believe in intense study, self-deprivation, and poverty. It is believed that through an ascetic lifestyle, adherents will come closer to God in this life rather than waiting for death and judgment. Unlike orthodox Islam, which focuses on studying the Quran and other literature to increase spiritual knowledge, Sufis believe that one can look inward and study with teachers rather than with literature to increase spiritual knowledge. Sufis often live lives of severe poverty as a way to break away from the world. Sufism varies from region to region but is practiced in almost all Arab countries in one form or another. Its most basic tenets revolve around the idea that through seeking God and living a life separate from the world, one can get closer to God in this life.

The Grand Sanusi was an educated religious scholar and a revivalist preacher. He argued that internal divisions within Islam were tearing it apart and that only a return to a pure form of Islam would lead to salvation and would also help build a stronger Islamic state. To propagate his ideas, he founded the first *zawaayaa* or guesthouse near Mecca in the 1830s, but local Ottoman officials opposed his policies and forced him to return to Cyrenaica. Back in Cyrenaica, he founded many guesthouses. The guesthouses were originally designed as travel lodges aimed at allowing travelers to rest on their journeys, but they quickly became centers for religious and political discussions.

The Grand Sanusi's blend of orthodoxy and Sufism appealed to the troubled region of Cyrenaica. He believed in the importance of hard work to make a living and did not allow his followers to dabble in fanaticism or to live in extreme poverty. Instead, they were to live lives that were simple, yet comfortable. They were required give away the portion of their income not needed to sustain comfortable, simple lifestyles. The Grand Sanusi blended the ideals of learning and seeking God in this world with the belief that Islam could become powerful against encroaching European values only if Muslims returned to true Islamic practices.

At the time of his death in 1859, the Grand Sanusi had succeeded in converting a large number of Bedouins. He also established a religious school in Jaghbub, an important town on the route to Mecca. The Grand Sanusi's belief in austere living, mysticism, and hard work appealed to the nomadic groups of Cyrenaica and allowed him to build a strong and powerful religious network. This network was later converted to political assets through which his sons ended the incessant Bedouin raids and encouraged trade and agriculture. The influence of the Sanusi Order spread south into Chad. Although the Italians defeated the Sanusi Order in the early 1900s, the Order became a powerful force for Libyan nationalism and the propagation of Islam during the Italian occupation.

As the resistance movement formed by the Sanusi Order against Italian occupation gained adherents, the element of religious devotion within the Order waned. In the 1930s, the Italians destroyed the religious and educational centers set up by the Sanusi Order, which led to the Order's demise. However, King Idris was a descendent of the Grand Sanusi, a fact that commanded great respect from the diverse parts of his kingdom.

Judaism

Until fairly recently, Libya was a home to arguably the oldest Jewish communities in the world, dating to as far back as 300 B.C. at which time Libyan Jews were a relatively large and prosperous community. During Roman rule, the Jews were primarily merchants and largely settled in Tripoli and Cyrene. The Jewish community in Cyrene staged an uprising against Roman rule. After the Romans reasserted their rule over Cyrene, they killed hundreds of Jews still living in Libya. During the Christian era, both Rome and Byzantium persecuted the Jews. Many Jews welcomed the Arabs' invasion in the eighth century as a way to escape Christian persecution. Under Ottoman rule, the Jews were allowed to practice their religion as long as they paid *jizya*, a tax non-Muslims paid to practice their faith and customs in peace.

Under Italian rule in the 1930s, Mussolini's government enforced harsh anti-Jewish laws in Libya. The Jews suffered a series of pogroms aimed at denying them access to power in Libya. Similar to the situation throughout Europe and the rest of the Mediterranean region, the 1940s was a difficult time for the Jewish community in Libya. The arrival of German troops in 1941 sounded the death knell for the Jewish community in Libya. In 1942, German soldiers destroyed Jewish communities throughout Libya and deported thousands of Jews. Many Jews died as they trekked across the desert. Many more were forced into slave labor camps, where thousands perished.

Between World War II and 1949, a few thousand Libyan Jews smuggled themselves into Israel. This ended in 1949 as the British government opened up Israel to Jewish immigration, which led to the immigration of over 30,000 Libyan Jews. This process would continue over the next couple of decades. When Qaddafi took power in 1969, there were fewer than 500 Jews in the entire country. He passed a series of repressive laws that, among other things, deprived Jews of the right to own property and released all debts owed the Jews. Qaddafi's repression accelerated Jewish flight and virtually ensured the final demise of Judaism in Libya. The Jewish population in Libya today is nonexistent.

Christianity

Although about 97 percent of Libya's population practices Islam, more than 100,000 Christians live in the country. Christianity arrived in North Africa, Libya inclusive, before Islam. The oldest Christian communities in North Africa were established around Oriental Orthodox churches. In the fourth century CE, the Ethiopian Orthodox Tewahedo Church, the Coptic Church of Egypt, and the Eritrean Orthodox Tewahedo Church rose to prominence in North Africa. Influential figures who would go on to play significant roles in the development and spread of Christianity outside of Africa originated from these North African Christian communities. Notable among these individuals were Origen Tertullian, Saint Augustine of Hippo, Saint Maurice, and three Roman Catholic popes: Victor I, Miltiades, and Gelasius I. Other important North African Christians include Simon of Cyrene and the famous Ethiopian eunuch baptized by Saint Philip the evangelist.

Virtually no documentary evidence exists to establish if an early Christian church existed in Libya. However, Christianity did exist in nearby Ethiopia and Egypt well before the reign of the great Christian King Ezana of Axum in the early fourth century. Theologians have argued that the numerous biblical and biblical historical references to "Ethiopians" generally referred to anyone from North Africa and not solely Ethiopians proper. Noted church historian Rufinus of Tyre recorded that when Frumentius and his companion Edesius were children, they were shipwrecked, captured, and carried away to Axum. A small community of Christians who had fled from Roman persecution and gained refuge and lived in Axum kindly received young Frumentius and Edesius. The two remained in Axum, where they were secretly promoting Christianity. Ironically, it was not the direct influence of Roman colonization but Libya's proximity to Rome and Egypt that most influenced the presence of a small, but strong, population of Catholic and Coptic Christian communities in modern Libya. It was illegal for Christians to preach and convert the Muslim population, but relations between these Christian minorities and their predominantly Muslim Libyan neighbors were agreeable.

Libya's more than 100,000 Christians are divided into three major denominations: the Coptics, Roman Catholics, and Anglicans. An estimated 60,000 Libyan Christians are Coptic. Forty thousand Roman Catholics are attended by two bishops: one in Tripoli and another in Benghazi. The Anglican population is rather smaller, primarily composed of African immigrants living in Tripoli. The Anglicans do have one small church that is administered by an Anglican Bishop who lives in Cairo.

Although Libya is an Islamic state, the relationship between Christians and Muslims is relatively stable. Christians are free to practice their religion, although there are a few restrictions. Christians are forbidden from proselytizing to the Muslim population. In addition, Muslims who convert to Christianity are arrested and imprisoned. When a male Christian marries a Muslim woman, he is required to convert to Islam. If a female Christian marries a Muslim man, she does not have to convert, but the children from such unions will be Muslims. So while the relationship between Christians and Muslims is amicable, there are certain requirements that Christians must abide by while living in a Muslim state.

In general, persons are rarely harassed on account of their religious beliefs unless such beliefs are believed to be politically inspired. In Libya, religious fanaticism and religious fundamentalism are discouraged, and the disapproval extends to Islam. The Libyan government is intolerant of fundamental Islam, which it regards as a danger to the government.

The Coptic Church

The Coptic Orthodox Church of Alexandria is one of the oldest Christian denominations in the world. The church is believed to have been founded by Apostle Mark in the middle of the first century. Coptic Christians were unified with the Christian churches of Europe until the Council of Chalcedon in 451 CE A doctrinal disagreement over the nature of Jesus led to the formation of a separate church. The Coptic Church faced serious persecution from the Roman Catholic and Eastern Orthodox Churches.

In 451, the Council of Chalcedon decreed that Jesus Christ has a dual nature: one human and the other divine. The Council of Chalcedon was attended by leading Christian scholars from around the world. The Coptic Church rejected this doctrine and argued that Christ has only one nature: a fusion of human and divine, both merging into a single nature. On the surface, the issues seemed a minor distinction in theology. However, the ramifications were enormous. By refusing to recognize the Pope's decree that Christ had two natures, the Coptic Church placed itself in direct opposition to European Christianity. In Coptic lore, the disagreement over the nature of Christ at the Council of Chalcedon was only an excuse for the Roman Catholic Church to eliminate one of its biggest rivals, the Coptic Church in Alexandria. The Roman Church had not yet consolidated its position as the preeminent church in Christendom by the time the council met in Chalcedon, and many Coptic Christians believe that Pope Leo I's rejection of the Coptic Church was a pretense to weaken the power of the Patriarch in Alexandria.

Notwithstanding the disagreement, Coptic Christianity became one of the major religions in the three regions of modern Libya. Today, Coptic Christians are a small religious minority in Libya. Libya's Coptic Church, like many other Orthodox churches in Eastern Europe and the Middle East, does not recognize the authority of the Roman Pope. Instead, the church looks toward the Patriarch in Alexandria for guidance and has its own religious leaders.

The Catholic Church in Libya

Catholic Christians in Libya are primarily immigrant workers from Malta and Italy. They reside in the major cities, particularly Tripoli and Benghazi. The Catholic Church, although small, does have a relatively strong following despite its history as an agent of imperial Italy. Many Libyans viewed the Catholic Church and Italy's attempt to force Catholicism on the nation as another force of domination. Libyans seem less suspicious of the Coptic Church, which has been in North Africa and Libya for almost 2,000 years.

Virtually all Catholic priests and nuns work in the main coastal cities. Most Catholic priests and nuns work in hospitals, particularly with the disabled. Catholic clergy and nuns are free to wear their religious dress in public. In addition to Catholic clergy and nuns, Coptic and Greek Orthodox priests also live and work in Tripoli and Benghazi.

In 1997, the Vatican established diplomatic relations with Libya because of the tens of thousands of Catholics living in Libya. The Vatican recognized that Libya had taken steps to safeguard freedom of religion. The ultimate goal behind the diplomatic overtures was to be more effective in protecting the interests of an estimated 100,000 Christians in Libya.

WORLDVIEWS

Importance of Work

Since the days of the Grand Sanusi, both religious and political leaders in Libya stressed the virtue of hard work. The influence of Mediterranean culture significantly moderated these earlier beliefs. For example, Libyans take daily siestas, but they do believe in hard work. Behind what appears to be an outward love of pleasure lies a belief that working hard is beneficial to the country, individuals, and God.

The culture of working hard can be attributed to the Sanusi Order's strict values of cooperation, intensive studying, austere life, and minimal acquisitions of property. In addition, religion and morality also exert strong pressure, and there are antitheft and anticorruption values applied to all aspects of life.

The Role of Government

Qaddafi successfully built a socialist state, as he promised during the Revolution in 1969. Until recently, private enterprise was virtually nonexistent in Libya; the Libyan government provided housing, food, healthcare, education, and, in some cases, even cars for citizens. Qaddafi's government attempted to provide Libyans with all of the things they needed. The government could provide these necessities because it controlled every key industry in the country.

Many Libyans had grown to view the government as their benefactor, and they invariably tolerated the government's excesses because it supplied all of their basic necessities. Opposition to Qaddafi's rule in Libya did exist, but he effectively controlled criticism through mass arrests, detentions, and periodic purges that targeted his opposition. He especially targeted opposition within the military. Above all, Qaddafi regarded himself as the only one who could save Libya from imperialist domination.

When he seized power in 1969, Qaddafi espoused Arabic socialism, and throughout his rule he implemented policies in line with his beliefs. Early in his reign, Qaddafi established laws against citizens holding private bank accounts. In 1979, the Libyan government ordered all Libyans to deposit their money in the national banks, citing the need to convert the currency to the newly introduced denominations. However, once citizens deposited their money, Qaddafi limited the amount of money they could withdraw from their accounts. Finally, in March 1980, the government outlawed holding any bank accounts and seized Libyans' savings. These acts forced Libyans to rely on the government for everything, as their savings were wiped out.

In addition to eliminating bank accounts, Qaddafi's government also passed laws limiting the number of cars and houses people could own. Throughout the 1970s, wealthy Libyans witnessed the seizure of their vacation and second homes and cars, which were then distributed among the highly favored officials in Qaddafi's government. In more recent times, private businesses flourished in Libya as the government relaxed its grip on the economy. Entrepreneurs were encouraged to invest in the Libyan economy.

Pan-Arabism

Pan-Arabism, or the belief in a unified Arab state, had been a powerful force in Libyan history. For instance, the Grand Sanusi and his followers used Pan-Arabism to mount an intense campaign against Italian rule. Pan-Arab Nationalism has been gaining in popularity ever since the fourth century. The most fundamental belief of Pan-Arabism is that all Arab nations should be unified into one large super-state.

Postcolonial Pan-Arabism found a ready advocate in Abel Nasser, the Egyptian leader. However, his efforts yielded little success, as the modalities for merger with other Arab nations proved to be one knotty issue that could not be solved. Following in the vein of Nasser, Qaddafi advocated for the union of all Arab states into one Arab nation. While most North African nations did not share in his belief in Pan-Arabism, almost certainly because none were willing to relinquish sovereignty to create a large Arab state, during the 1970s and 1980s, Qaddafi did attempt to merge Libya with other Arab nations in North Africa.

In addition to Pan-Arabism, Qaddafi also advocated for Pan-Islamism, the concept of a free union of all Islamic countries and peoples. Following Nasser's death on September 28, 1970, Qaddafi took up the ideological leadership of Arab nationalism and proclaimed a Federation of Arab Republics. The Republic was comprised of Libya, Egypt, and Syria. The merger broke down in 1972 as the three nations disagreed on the precise terms of the union. Not willing to give up on the idea, in 1974, Qaddafi signed an agreement with Habib Bourguiba of Tunisia for a union between their two countries. Like the Republic, this effort also collapsed and ultimately degenerated into strong animosity between the two countries. After the second disappointment, Qaddafi shifted his attention to creating a United States of Africa.

In modern usage, the term "Pan-Arabism" is usually understood as support of and solidarity between Arab states on issues of common interest. Arab nationalism is nevertheless a powerful tool in Libyan ideology. Libya identifies more closely with Arab concerns, such as the Israeli and Palestinian conflict, than it does with African issues.

Pan-Africanism

Libya is an African state. As such, Qaddafi also embraced the goals of Pan-Africanism, a belief that all Africans around the world are linked. Pan-Africanism has its roots in the nineteenth-century African diaspora, particularly within continental America. People of African descent in the Americas looked to Africa as a homeland that they had been taken away from, and one to which they still felt a strong connection. By the early twentieth century, Pan-Africanism had taken on a new dimension in which people identified less with Africa as a continent as with Africans as a people. The Pan-African movement gained strength through the 1950s as a response to European colonialism and a growing belief that Africans should work together to improve the continent.

When Qaddafi came to power, he looked toward the rest of Africa as an avenue for his version of anti-imperialism. Like the Sanusiyya during the nineteenth century, one of Qaddafi's primary concerns was liberating African countries from colonial rule. Qaddafi's Libya became an active and important supporter of African liberation movements throughout Africa. Zimbabweans, Namibians, South Africans, Angolans, Mozambicans, and many others traveled to Libya to receive money, training, and weapons. Qaddafi's Libya played an active role in the Organization of African Unity, particularly on its Liberation Committee. After many of his schemes to create a unified Arab state failed, he began to look more and more toward creating a unified Africa, and he provided aid in addition to political leverage to many African states. In 2009, Libya was awarded the chairmanship of the African Union, the successor to the Organization of African Unity.

Throughout the last decade, Qaddafi pushed for the formation of a United States of Africa. In Qaddafi's view, the division of Africa into many countries was preventing it from facing rest of the world as a strong continent ready to meet the challenges of globalization. He believed the socioeconomic and political crises facing different African nations resulted from the fragmented nature of the continent. He persuaded African leaders to support a continental government as a way to fashion a new Africa. Qaddafi's proposal was ambitious given the fact that some African nations were small and had uncertain futures. However, a critical look at Qaddafi's proposal reveals that it provided almost no real chance for continental unification.

It is doubtful that a United States of Africa would create a unified federation of all African states and that it would bolster the Organization of African Unity and the African Union. Although Africa has the resources and the population to make a Pan-African nation viable, ethnic diversity and serious issues of unequal socioeconomic and political growth and development in the different African states make the option difficult to put into practice. In addition, few nations would give up their sovereignty for promises of future wealth, especially those African nations that are already stable and prosperous.

Considering Qaddafi's record as a radical revolutionary and a staunch Islamic socialist, it is easy to question the legitimacy of his motives. For instance, in his *Green Book*, Qaddafi espoused strong Pan-Islamic and Pan-Arab nationalistic tendencies that are radically opposed to the religious and cultural sentiments of most peoples and groups in Africa. In Nigeria, he openly advocated that Muslims should consider killing Christians who stood in the way of the spread of Islam. Qaddafi's actions in Nigeria when compared with his call for Pan-Africanism reflect that his motives were not entirely altruistic. In Libya in particular and in North Africa in general, Qaddafi advocated that Arabic language and culture should be culturally, linguistically, socially, politically, ideologically, and economically blended to ensure the survival of Arabs. His advocacy for Pan-Islamism and Pan-Arabism undoubtedly presupposed the imposition of Islamic and Arabic religion, language, culture, morals, and ethos on other Africans. His support of Pan-Africanism was a subterfuge for Islamizing and Arabizing Africa as a whole and, potentially, other countries as well.

In 2009, Qaddafi assembled several African kings and had himself crowned the King of African Traditional Kings. It is clear that Qaddafi portrayed himself as a leader of Africa and, therefore, a firm believer in Pan-Africanism. However, like most Libyans, he regarded himself as Arab and part of the Arab world—not as an African and part of the African world. Libyans' intolerance of African immigrant workers is telling proof of this hypocrisy.

Relationship with the West

Libya's relationship with the West is complicated. The effects of Italian colonialism are still fresh; many older Libyans can still recall the terrible suffering they experienced at the hands of the colonial government. When Qaddafi came to power, he condemned imperialism. He also roundly dismissed all western nations and their interests in Libya and Africa as part of their quest for world domination.

His support of terrorism and his disagreement with Israel clouded Libya's relationship with the West for decades. The United States believed that by ejecting Westerners from Libya in the early 1970s, Qaddafi was opening the door to the former Soviet Union. Subsequent events revealed this fear was unwarranted. Qaddafi viewed the former Soviet Union with as much suspicion as he did the United States; the former Soviet Union was also an imperial power bent on world domination. Qaddafi had few problems accepting Soviet military equipment, but he severely limited the role that the Soviets could play in Libyan affairs.

Libya and the United States

Libya has had a long and tumultuous relationship with the United States. After Qaddafi took power in 1969, the relationship between the two countries steadily deteriorated (with the exception of the last few years). Within the last five years, Libya entered into the comity of nations after years of existing as a pariah, and the United States and Libya have slowly began normalizing their relationship.

Libya's interactions with the United States began in the early years of the nineteenth century. During this time, the Pasha of Tripoli gained great wealth by raiding American and European vessels off the coast of Libya. Most European nations paid tributes to Tripoli to spare themselves the expense and difficulty of raids. Prior to American independence, American merchants had been protected by the tribute England paid the Libyans. However, after declaring independence in 1776, English payments no longer covered U.S. shipping, and Libya began to demand payments from American merchants. Thomas Jefferson refused to pay tribute to the Pasha of Tripoli and chose to go to war to protect American shipping. Jefferson ordered the navy to the Mediterranean to defeat Tripoli's navy. On arrival, the Tripolitanians seized the *Philadelphia*, a 36 gun U.S. Navy frigate. Before they could take the ship away, the captain of a nearby U.S. ship sank the frigate to prevent Tripoli from taking it.

After this embarrassing defeat, U.S. Marines succeeded in landing on the coast of Tripoli and advanced toward the city. Before they could attack, a cease-fire was declared, and hostilities ended. The United States paid the Pasha of Tripoli a ransom to recover captured Americans and to guarantee that future American ships would be spared. Libya's relationship with the United States collapsed until the end of World War II.

Libya's location along the Mediterranean gave it a strategic position in the emerging Cold War. After World War II, Libya's Italian rulers were forced to leave the fate of North Africa and Libya to the United Nations. The United States and Great Britain, fearing the Soviet Union's interest in Libya, pushed for Libya to become an independent nation with close ties to western governments. After the establishment of the United Kingdom of Libya, the United States strove to keep Libya within the West's sphere of influence and away from the Soviet Union. Britain and America set up military bases in Libya.

Following Libya's independence, the U.S. military was primarily concerned with keeping its Wheelus Air Force Base, which the United States saw as vital in any future conflict with the former Soviet Union. In exchange for the base, the United States invested heavily in Libya. However, this money often went into the hands of American companies or the elites surrounding the monarchy. Ordinary Libyans saw little of the benefits that came from massive amounts of American investment and were skeptical of American interests in Libya.

Although a large number of Americans lived in Libya either as military personnel or as civilians working in American companies, Americans and Libyans remained separate within the country and viewed each other with hostility. Most Libyans resented the arrogance of American service personnel and civilian contractors, and wanted them out of Libya. Coupled with growing economic discontent, the presence of foreign military and civilian workers led to the downfall of the Sanusi monarchy and helped usher in the reign of Qaddafi.

After the One September Revolution of 1969, Qaddafi pushed for Arab Socialism and an end to what he considered U.S. and British imperialism. Concerned about its military base and its companies in Libya, the United States wanted to know Qaddafi's intentions and if he would respect the country's obligations to the United States. After stabilizing Libya's government, Qaddafi forced the United States and Great Britain to remove their forces from Libyan airfields and declared the day they left as a national holiday.

Abdelbaset al-Megrahi, who was found guilty of the 1988 Lockerbie bombing, left, and son of the Libyan leader Seif al-Islam Qadaffi, right, gesture on his arrival at an airport in Tripoli, Libya. (AP Photo, File)

When he nationalized all private and public companies, institutions, and infrastructure in Libya, which included taking over many American businesses, primarily those in the oil industry, he also reorganized the economy. Qaddafi's new economic policy and support of violence in liberation struggles in and around Africa quickly strained Libya's relationship with the United States. Qaddafi became an outspoken critic of imperialism, and he channeled money and weapons into many liberation movements throughout the world. The United States considered some of those liberation movements terrorism. The Carter and Reagan administrations viewed Libya as a state sponsor and supporter of global terrorism, and they relied on sanctions and other actions to economically and politically isolate Libya from the rest of the world.

Reagan administration sanctions in 1983 and bombings in 1986 led to a suspension of all contact between the two nations. Libya's economy, which had boomed during the oil crisis of the 1970s and 1980s, faltered as a result of the sanctions. By the 1980s, the United States and Libya had no official relationship, and conditions had deteriorated to such an extent that Reagan ordered the U.S. Air Force to bomb Libya in hopes of killing Qaddafi. The diplomatic policies of subsequent administrations were hostile and based on the belief that Qaddafi threatened world peace. Currently, many U.S. companies, particularly oil companies, operate in Libya, and the relationship between the two countries has improved.

After the September 11, 2001, terrorist attacks on the World Trade Center and Pentagon, Qaddafi became a supporter of the war on terror and subsequently re-established relations with the United States. For example, travel restrictions were lifted, and tensions between the two countries cooled. However, while in power, Qaddafi remained suspicious of capitalism and U.S. interests even though relations between the two nations are had improved in the new millennia.

3

Literature and Media

LITERATURE

GENERALLY, LIBYAN LITERATURE HAS BEEN DESCRIBED as being very recent and essentially laced with anti-Italian colonization themes. On the one hand, these views construe Libyan literature narrowly, limiting it to only literature than is written; they discount the rich repertoires of Berber and Tuareg oral literature. While a large body of oral literature still exists in Libya, much effort is required to translate it from Arabic into other languages to attract a wider readership. On the other hand, these views take no notice of the timeless contributions of Libyan prose writers and lyric poets to Greco-Roman literature. The Ancient Greek lyric poet Callimachus, the exquisite prose stylist Sinesius, and more than a hundred other literary luminaries who contributed immensely to Greek literature were Libyans. In fact, many of Aesop's fables have been classified as part of the Libyan tales and literary tradition. Classicists have recognized that modern Arab and African literature have had little or no contribution from Libyans due largely to Qaddafi's persecution of writers and artists. In contrast, Ancient Greek and Roman literature benefited immensely from the works of Libyans. Indeed, Egyptian literary contributors were summarily described in classical literature as simply Libyans.

In addition to contributing to classical Greek and Roman literature, Tuareg and Bedouin poets and singers composed and spread poems that became very popular, for example, *huda*, or the camel driver's song. Bedouin and Tuareg women are distinguished by their songs, which delight audiences at festivals, fairs, and ceremonies. Berber and Tuareg griots and bards utilize characteristic African rhythms in their oral tradition. As noted earlier, much of this great literature is in Arabic, and much work will be required to translate them into other languages.

Most Libyan literature is oral in form and, therefore, far removed from nonspeakers of Arabic or African languages. However, this inadequacy and the limitations it imposes are not adequate grounds to deny the existence of a rich Libyan literary culture or to ignore its contributions to the literary world.

Contrary to generally held beliefs, contemporary Libyan literature is not solely about Italian colonization and oppression but generally includes stories about the life experiences of everyday people within their socioeconomic and political spaces under both foreign and indigenous rule. Whether urban or rural, Libyan literature owes much to the rich sociocultural heritages of Libya and Africa and to a cacophony of heritages including the Greeks, Romans, Arabs, Spaniards, and Italians. In other words, the history of contemporary Libyan literature is a judicious blend of Berber, Bedouin, and Tuareg poetry, folk tales, and proverbs and recollections of the difficult experiences of injustice, tyranny, and oppression suffered by ordinary Libyans in the hands of the various groups who have occupied and ruled Libya over the years, including Qaddafi.

The classical poet Ovid once noted that oppression, tyranny, and adversity spawn great poetry. Some Libyan literature does explore the brutality associated with Italian occupation, but it remains to be seen if this theme will appear in future literature given the recent revolution that deposed Qaddafi. The oppression and brutality mounted against writers and artists in Libya under Qaddafi stifled opposition and led many writers to censor their work because Qaddafi targeted any writings and writers that he felt antagonized him and his government. Understandably, opposition literature against Qaddafi within Libya was rare, but some Libyan writers did openly criticize Qaddafi verbally and in writing.

Although Arabs dominated the political and cultural values of Libya for over a thousand years, their influences on Libyan literature are largely limited to the language and styles but not content. Indigenous poetry, African folktales, witty sayings, and proverbs suffuse contemporary Libyan literature. However, the influences of Arab literature were greatest during the Abbasid and Umayyad Caliphates when Arab culture spread from the Middle East to the Atlantic Ocean, from Pakistan to Turkey. During this period, Libya, like all of North Africa, was not immune to Arab influences. While this Arabic literature focused primarily on the events surrounding the time, it is fundamentally religious in content and is in the form of praise poetry and other forms of worship.

In most of North Africa, Libya inclusive, Arabic literature merged with indigenous Tuareg, Berber, and Bedouin literature, which was typically short stories and poems. Scholars have argued that short stories and poems comprised the body of indigenous Libyan literature and that novel and book-length works did not develop until very recently. This development reflects the nomadic nature of Libyan society. Traditionally nomadic peoples' literature is in the form of poems and short stories that reflect lives on the move versus those of more sedentary people like those of, say, West Africa. Larger works require time and space to compose, two requirements that the nomadic groups of Libya lacked. Hence, indigenous literature took forms that could be memorized and passed on orally from one group to another. It is therefore commonplace for griots, bards, poets, and storytellers to travel from one community to another telling stories and reciting poems of the day to rapt audiences.

In the twentieth century, rising Arab nationalism altered the nature of Libyan literature, forcing it to adopt a combative posturing, especially against Italian colonialism. It also espoused Pan-Arabism rather than traditional values that dominated traditional Libyan lore; Arab nationalism could not alter the traditional form of Libyan literature to longer book-length works of prose or poetry. In fact, more than ever before, Arab nationalism influenced Libyan poetry; poets wrote to defy colonial rulers and to express nationalist sympathies.

Poetry

Undoubtedly, poetry is one of the most popular literary traditions of Libya. In rural Libya, short poems are sung with accompanying musical instruments by traveling theatre groups. The exploits of heroes and heroines are sung daily and serve as useful medium for instilling courage, nationalism, and community feeling. Along with the influence of Arab literature, poetic themes have expanded to include poems of praise and worship which are used primarily in religious gatherings.

Resistance Poetry

As noted previously, Libyan literature, especially poetry, has undergone a series of transitions over the years. While traditional Libyan poetry is still popular, especially in rural areas, contemporary Libyan writers and composers developed unique poetic forms and themes that emerged during the Italian colonial occupation. This literature reflected anticolonial themes. Libya witnessed a flowering of resistance poetry between 1950 and 1960.

This poetry is characterized by patriotic zeal and protests against the continuing Western presence in Libya, a presence that continued even after independence. The poets and composers railed against the military presence of the United States and Great Britain, and against other Western economic interests in Libya. Oftentimes, poets and composers focused on King Idris's government for "selling out" the young nation in return for the "poisoned crumbs" of Western aid. During that period, as today, poetry readings were held throughout the country and were often broadcast over the radio and television.

Resistance poetry, with its emphasis on protesting foreign rule and Western influences on Libya, emerged as early as the 1920s. Poets Rafiq al-Muhdawi, Al Usta Omar, Ahmed al Sharif, and many others championed the patriotic and political tone and content of resistance poetry. Focusing on the brutality associated with the Italian occupation, these poets decried the harsh impact of colonialism on Libya, and they used poetry to express anticolonial sentiment and to encourage Libyan nationalists in their resistance against Italian occupation. Given the brutality associated with Italian rule in Libya, the danger associated with open protests was not lost on Libyan poets. Therefore, many of them turned to the oral medium and to Arabic and African languages for the transmission of their literature. Even so, many resistance poets spent time in Italian jails.

Jails and suppression would eventually erode the progress of Libyan resistance literature for a time; during the closing days of Italian occupation, this type of literature was largely silent. However, jails and suppression can hold off for only a short while resistance poetry with its themes of resistance and politics. The end of World War II and ushered in a period of optimism for the future of Libya. Many of the writers and poets who had been driven into exile in Egypt, Syria, and Lebanon returned to Libya. From 1951 and into the 1960s, resistance poetry once again resurfaced. The poets and writers of the 1950s included Kamel Maghur, Ibrahim Fagih, and Bashir Hashimi. They had not forgotten the harsh realities of Italian rule, and works about Italian colonialism flourished immediately after Libya became independent.

Libyan literature bloomed with the writings of Sadeq al-Neihum, Khalifa al-Fakhri, Kamel Maghur, Muhammad al-Shaltami, and Ali al-Regeie. These and many other Libyan writers adopted nationalist, socialist, and generally progressive views of their nation. Most works focused primarily on British and American oil companies and military, whose influences were described as attacks on Libya's future and potential. The writers and poets cast Britain, the United States, and Jews as outsiders and a drain on the fortunes of Libya.

Libyan nationalists were concerned about the influences of Great Britain and the United States over Libya and felt that King Idris was selling out to the West. By the 1960s, British and American military bases in Libya became the focus of literary criticism. Ali al-Regeie's poem "Flameless Candles," written in 1966, aptly epitomized this new wave of resistance literature:

> What can rain do to barren land?
> Only the thorns of these cursed cactus spreading over the land
> I wish these blindfolded eyes could desire to see the light of day
> I wish these blindfolded eyes could cry.[1]

Resistance poets argued that relations with the Americans and British had blinded the rather young nation and prevented it from realizing its full potential. The poets reminded Libyans of the labors of their past heroes and heroines who fought and died to obtain independence; many of those heroes and heroines were driven into silence under King Idris's new government. The Americans and the British exploited not only Libya on a daily basis, the poets argued, but also other Western powers for their own benefit. Resistance poems rallied and mobilized Libyans to stand up, fight for their rights, defend their land, and reimagine their futures in an egalitarian country.

Literature in Post-1969 Libya

The criticisms against King Idris fomented the 1969 military coup that brought Colonel Qaddafi to power. Although poets criticized King Idris for courting Western powers to develop the impoverished young nation, he neither persecuted nor jailed writers and poets. However, by mid-1970s, the Qaddafi-led government banned private printing and publishing, and, in their stead, the government set up a single publishing house. Libyan poets and authors were thereby compelled to publish their works with the government. In real terms, this constituted the worst form of censorship; writers and poets were compelled to write favorably and in support of the new Qaddafi-led government. Literature was considered a critical part of nation-building, and Qaddafi believed it must present what the government wanted the people to know. Writers like Kamel Maghur and Ahmed Fagih, who had dominated the literary landscape of the 1950s and 1960s, continued to write, but others refused government orders and were imprisoned, forced to flee, or compelled to cease writing altogether.

Literature in post-1969 Libya became a form of propaganda and indoctrination; pro-government literature dominated the Libyan literary world. Despite Qaddafi's iron grip on Libya's literary world, writers and poets turned to new genres to carry their messages. Stories of anthropomorphized animals in an equally anthropomorphized world served as vehicles for social criticism. As censorship laws cascaded down from Tripoli during the 1970s, resistance poetry began to turn against the One September Revolution, and the Qaddafi began to crack down on intellectuals who opposed him. For instance, in 1978, government secret police arrested writers and poets who had gathered for a poetry reading. These writers and poets spent many years in prison. Arrests and detentions did not diminish the skills of these writers and poets; rather these circumstances honed them. For example, Omar Al-Kikli, a writer jailed by Qaddafi, recently published a series of poems and short stories about his days in prison. Literary production stalled as a result of arrests and detention; persecution forced poets and writers to become more self-conscious and self-censoring of their own works.

"Awareness," one of Al-Kikli's poems, documents his experiences under Qaddafi's tyrannical rule but also expresses discontent about Libya's sad state of affairs. Al-Kikli wrote:

> The soft sunlight that was covering the yard stung his eyes.
> He raised his head, shading his face with his palm, gazing at the sky.
> Its remoteness and blueness, which loomed deliciously, astonished him.[2]

In this poem, Al-Kikli described his incarceration as painful. He was unable to see daylight, unable to enjoy life, and unable to even observe the beauty of the sky. The poem indicts Libya's leadership and condemns attempts to silence critical voices as taking away people's freedom and killing their spirits. In many other poems, Libyan poets and writers showed the dynamic ways through which political prisoners, poets, and writers survived Qaddafi's prisons and authoritarianism. Although Libyan prison poetry is a recent development, it represents a shift in the Libyan resistance poetry tradition.

Recent Poets

In the 1990s, Qaddafi loosened but did not abolish the censorship laws. This détente led to a literary revival. Poetry recitations and competitions resumed, and many publishing ventures opened. In addition, English and French books were allowed, and many bookshops offering American novels opened up in major cities and towns in Libya. Despite these concessions, books censorship remained, and writers and poets were forced to continue self-censoring their works. Notwithstanding this, some measure of dissent was expressed in contemporary Libyan literature. In addition, Libya's male-dominated literary universe became democratized, and some female writers have emerged, most of whom are in their late twenties and early thirties. Notable examples of women writers include Laila Neihoum, Najwa Ben Shetwan, and Maryam Salama.

In addition to the emergence of female writers, foreign-born Libyan writers, most notably Ibrahim Al-Kouni, Ahmad Al-Faqih, and Sadeq al-Neihum, have also contributed significantly to Libyan literature. Khaled Mattawa, a New York–based Libyan poet, remains the most popular of this category of Libyan writers and poets. Mattawa's poetry focuses on borderlands and the way multicultural communities interact. In one of his poems, "East of Carthage," he examined the anguish of illegal African immigrants who use Libya as a gateway to Europe. Ashur Etwebi, a poet and college professor in Tripoli, focused primarily on Libya's past and the various groups that helped shape the nation's past. While Mattawa was able to engage Libya and Africa's problems directly, Etwebi's presence within Libya compelled him to focus on issues that would avoid Qaddafi's spotlight.

Other writers contributed to the Libyan literary tradition by leaving Libya for other countries with less restrictive laws to the practice of their arts, but they often faced similar censorship for their provocative political ideas. For example, Idris Ali, an Egyptian novelist, won the Best Egyptian Novelist award in 1999. Hosni Mubarak banned his last work, *The Leader is Getting a Haircut*, less than four months after its publication. Mubarak's government seized the book, which was published in late 2009, at the Cairo International Book Fair and banned it in January 2010. Ali based the 130-page book on his four years' experiences as a foreign worker in Libya. Ali used the experiences of Egyptians working under inhumane conditions in Libya as a microcosm of what African labor migrants faced in Qaddafi's Libya. The Arabic Network for Human Rights Information (ANHRI) noted that the book chronicled not just the experiences of African labor migrants but also the social life and repression of Libyans under Qaddafi. Not only was Ali's book banned, his publisher was also arrested. Ali died in November 2010.

Before formally banning Ali's book, the Egyptian state strongly "rebuked" him for writing and publishing substance it considered subversive and insulting to Qaddafi. Prior to Ali's treatment at the hands of Egyptian authorities, in 2006, a female blogger in Alexandria was forced to quit blogging when Egypt's State Security Investigations Section asked her to delete a post critical of Colonel Qaddafi or risk arrest. The Section threatened that if she reported the matter to any human rights organization or to the press, she risked being killed.

Colonial and early postcolonial resistance literature was characterized by anticolonization and nationalistic themes; contemporary Libyan literature is dominated by local lore, North African and Eastern Mediterranean Arab literatures, and world literature at large. More than anything, Qaddafi's control of publishing affected Libya's literary production and contributed to the impression that Libyans made little contribution to global literary production. Today, traditional and resistance poetry and short stories remain popular despite Qaddafi's earlier prohibitions.

Following Qaddafi's fall from power and death, Libyan literature has shown enormous potential to grow and change in focus. For instance, the uprising against Qaddafi's regime stimulated new forms of music and a previously unseen level of cooperation between musicians and poets within Libya and between Libyan exiles around the world. The music of the Arab Spring expressed Libyans' desire for democracy and focused on themes of redemption, perseverance, and justice. The music of the Arab Spring is in both Arabic and English. One of the most popular songs is the rock ballad by Jasmine Ikanovic and Hussein Kablan entitled "We Will Never Surrender." Music of the Arab Spring is a testament to the fortitude and sacrifice of Libyans as they engaged Qaddafi forces for more than six months. The music inspired Libyans, at home and abroad, to continue their resistance.

In the past decade, the visibility of Libyan writers and poets increased within literary circles around the world. As more and more literary works were translated into English, consumption of Libyan literature widened, and initiatives evolved to showcase Libyan literature. Three Libyan-authored books (Ibrahim al-Koni's *The Animists*, Ahmed Fagih's *Gardens of the Night*, and Khalifa Hussein Mustapha's *Eye of the Sun*) were recently featured on the Arab Writers Union's list of the top 105 works of Arab literature of the last century. Except for al-Koni's work, which was written in English, the others were translated from Arabic to English.

Collections such as *The Bleeding of the Stone* and *The Seven Veils of Seth* and dozens of other short stories and poems by Ibrahim Al-Koni are today available in over 30 languages and have been widely recognized as excellent examples of desert literature. Al-Koni is a Libyan Tuareg who lives in Switzerland. Tuareg life in the desert and their contacts with the outside world inform Al-Koni's works. For instance, Asouf, the main character in *The Bleeding Stone*, is a wise sage outsiders depend on to understand the ways and history of the Bedouins. He is also the only one who knows the location of the *moufflan*, a wild and nearly extinct sheep that thrives only in the region. The book chronicles Asouf's journey of self-discovery as he interacts with two hunters who wish to kill the *moufflan*.

A few other Libyans have also achieved some prominence, most notably Libyan-American poet Khaled al-Mattawa and Libyan-British novelist Hisham Matar, who was shortlisted for the Man Booker Prize in 2006 for his *In the Country of Men*. Tunisia's annual literary festival, the Banipal, recently featured works by al-Koni, Matar, and Fagih. Al-Koni and Matar both have recently published novels in English: Matar's *Anatomy of a Disappearance* and Fagih's short story, *Sea Locusts*. Female writers, such as Razan

Naim Moghrabi, have recently published five collections of short stories and two novels. Moghrabi was considered for the International Prize for Arabic Fiction for 2011 for her *Women of Wind*, which focuses on the theme of female friendship and the secret lives of women. Libyan literature has also been featured recently in Words without Borders, Swiss-Libyan Art Project, Beirut 39, and other venues.

Bedouin Poetry

Despite globalization and increasing modernity, Bedouin poetry remains an important part of life for Bedouin communities throughout North Africa. The poetry of the nomadic groups is dominated mostly by women, is mostly geared toward entertainment, and provides an escape from the demanding and harsh life of the desert. Poets and those who are able to recall and retell stories and poems are highly valued in Bedouin society. These storytellers command great crowds as families and whole community turn out to hear them perform their works.

Unlike in most Libyan literary traditions, Bedouin women are not only significantly involved in reciting poems but also in composing them. Poetry has allowed Bedouin women a place of power and influence in what was a traditionally patriarchal society. The recitation process enables the transmission of culture and the circulation of current information, and its veiled criticism of those in power. In addition, recitations bring families together; children and adults, men and women interact as they enjoy their leisure.

Short Stories

As noted previously, short stories, owing to their brevity, are more amenable to a nomadic life where constant movement and temporary living structures characterizes life and living. Following poetry, short stories are the second most popular form of literature in Libya. The rise of short stories, like poetry, flourished during the Italian occupation of Libya in the 1920s. The brutality associated with Italian occupation helped unify Libyans and allowed them to aggregate around common issues such as colonization and independence, themes that feature prominently in all Libyan literary traditions. Like poetry, the themes of most short stories deal with everyday life, especially life under tyrannical rules—first of Italian colonizers and later of Colonel Qaddafi.

For the most part, short story writers focus on the society and the everyday problems Libyans faced as their daily negotiations with state actors, government, and groups within Libya. During the colonial period, these writers were concerned with resistance and a desire to describe the horrors of colonialism. Following independence, the focus shifted from foreign overlords to their indigenous replacements who ruled like colonial overlords. Many writers were critical of the Libyan government, especially King Idris's obtuse fascination with Western powers. With the discovery and commercial exploration of crude oil and subsequent Libyan wealth, storytellers did not relent in their criticisms of the government and its romance with foreigners, which they felt largely benefitted only the elite while ordinary Libyans were left to wallow in abject poverty.

Libyan writers feel their responsibility is to express the hopes, aspirations, and disappointments of the common people as they relate to their government while at the same time showing the strength, opportunities, and influence of the people. Libyan short stories do not shy away from any of these themes. They encapsulate the conflicts between individuals, traditional Libyan society, and constituted authority. Above all, Libyan short stories project the importance of groups and families in the overall survival of the country.

The theme of conflict became important as Libya emerged from the shackles of colonialism and joined the community of nations. Along with exploring conflicts between individuals and groups, conflicts between the traditional and modern became important to Libyan writers. They attempted to reconcile the rapid pace of development and progress with the struggle to maintain a traditional Libyan society.

Although all Libyan short stories attempt to capture various elements in Libyan society, in the main, Libyan short stories have four main styles: emotional, tell-a-tale, realistic, and analytical. Emotional stories were among the earliest types of stories in the short story genre to emerge, and they focused primarily on themes of unattainable love and on the goals and aspirations of the nation. Some of these stories narrate meetings between men and women that end in disaster and disappointment, and are, therefore, laced with a sense of grief and frustration. Tell-a-tale stories attempt to recapture Libya's glorious past and are, therefore, grounded in tradition and history. The stories are often filled with folktales and include supernatural elements.

In realistic stories, authors recapture the suffering of ordinary people under either colonial rule or exploitative capitalism. The characters in the stories suffer at the hands of foreigners who put them to work for little wages and steal the resources of the country. Finally, analytical stories are concerned mainly with the inner workings of individuals as they confront everyday problems and the larger structural issues happening in society. For example, in Kamel al-Maqhor's "Crying," a young boy named Omran tries to make sense of developments in his hometown and internalizes the struggle of ordinary Libyans, particularly their fears and sense of helplessness, as they grapple with the transition to industrialization. Al-Maqhor uses Omran to analyze the costs of modernization on Libyans. On his way to school, Omran witnesses a bulldozer moving back and forth along a road threatening to destroy a house and grocery store on either side. He wishes the "mechanical earthworm" would break down and spare the once beautiful landscape the destruction and devastation that inevitably follow industrialization. Omran represents any Libyan grappling with fundamental changes witnessed within Libyan society that result from the widening of the economy and from the rise in urbanization and the attendant social ills created by industrialization.

Novels

As noted previously, Qaddafi placed severe restrictions on book writing until the 1990s, which negatively impacted the production of book-length writings in Libya. However, since the 1990s, some Libyan authors have incorporated novels, along with traditional poems and short stories, into the literary tradition of the region. Like poetry and short stories, Libyan novels also focus on the theme of oppression and portray the conflicts that ordinary Libyans face as they navigate through the society. Three of the most widely read novels inside and outside Libya are *Hunger Has Other Faces* by Wafa Bu'esa, *In the Country of Men* by Hisham Matar, and *Gardens of the Night* by Ahmad Faquih.

The public received these three books differently, although all consider recurring themes of hope and desperation, themes prevalent in Libyan writings. *Hunger Has Other Faces* caused widespread controversy in Libya; many criticized its theme as anti-Islam. *In the Country of Men* and the *Gardens of the Night* grapple with the problems of contemporary Libya, and they enjoyed wider support and engendered more positive critiques than *Hunger Has Other Faces*.

Bu'esa published *Hunger Has Other Faces* in 2006. It examines the role of women in an Islamic society like Libya's. The main character is a young girl who flees Libya to Egypt, where she befriends a Coptic Christian and converts to Christianity. Following her conversion, she begins to view Islam as a repressive religion and the Coptic Church, by contrast, as a receptive and open one. Bu'esa's book was viewed by many as an attack on not only Libyan society but on Islam. *Hunger Has Other Faces* has struck a chord in many Libyans, creating many comments on blogs, protests, and official criticism. Whether Bu'esa's book mirrors the general sentiment of a few or of the entire populace is less important than whether it reflects the Libyan literary tradition of criticizing society and demonstrating how individuals navigate through the hurdles of life in a changing world.

Matar published *In the Country of Men* in 2006, and it has been compared to George Orwell's *1984*. Suleiman, the main character in the book, is a nine-year-old boy whose father and a neighbor were active in the university protests against the Libyan government in the 1980s. Matar's novel captures the impact of Qaddafi's political oppression through the eyes of Suleiman. Clearly critical of Qaddafi and his secret police, Suleiman's father and other critics disappear, and their families became increasingly isolated. Matar questions why Qaddafi would promise revolutionary changes in Libya but then turn it into a fiery furnace. The book was not available in Libya during Qaddafi's rule. It greatly impacted Britain's relationship with Libya, and increasing numbers of human rights groups began demanding the release of political prisoners, particularly Matar's father, whose whereabouts were not known during Qaddafi's ignoble rule.

Fagih published *Gardens of the Night* in 1995. The novel focuses on the theme of hopelessness and the struggles that life in Qaddafi's Libya entailed. The main character suffers a mental breakdown and wanders into the desert, where he has visions of a perfect city. However, even in this perfect city, he feels unsatisfied. The main character recognizes the deceits and contradictions that characterize the perfect city.

Unlike the two other authors, Ahmed Fagih lives and works in Libya, which influences the conservative tone of his novel. Fagih is a prolific author with dozens of poems, short stories, novels, and plays to his credit; he is a leading scholar on Libyan literature. Fagih heads many cultural organizations within Libya and has represented Libya at conferences and summits throughout the world. He serves as a model for upcoming Libyan writers and poets. His novel is a biting criticism of Qaddafi's government, but it also serves as a criticism of tyrannical governments all over the world, which contributes to the books popularity around the world.

The Future of Libyan Literature

Even before Qaddafi's death, a new dawn had risen in Libyan literature. In 2000, Qaddafi began releasing writers and intellectuals who had been detained (often without trials), and since then, a revival of Libyan literature has occurred. The growth of printing and publishing reflects this revival. Under Qaddafi's rule, authors were still unable to openly use traditional motifs of resistance that criticized the government, but Libyan authors were able to produce new and engaging works, despite government censorship.

The Internet, blogs, social media, online publishing, and privately owned traditional printing presses created new forums for writers and authors; all of these avenues undermined state-run printing presses during the Qaddafi years. With Qaddafi removed from power, the world waits for a burgeoning Libyan literary culture. Many literary works that were hidden for fear of persecution are set to be released. Hitherto hidden and oppressed talents will likely find an open, welcoming, and less restrictive Libya waiting for their work.

MEDIA

Just as Qaddafi banned private publishing from 1969 until 2006, all private media were banned under Qaddafi. All media outlets, including *Al-Shames Daily Newspaper, Al-Jamahirya Daily Newspaper, Al-Fajr Aljadeed Daily Newspaper,* and *Azzahf Alakhder Daily Newspaper,* were owned and operated by the Libyan government through the Jamahiriya News Agency. The newspapers are written in Arabic and served as official mouthpieces of Qaddafi's government. The official newspapers reported only news that satisfied the government. No reporter or writer dared criticize the government's conduct or how those in the government discharged their duties; anything construed as antigovernment inevitably attracted arrest, police brutality, and subsequent imprisonment, if not death. Foreign newspapers were available in major cities in Libya, although they were often out of date.

The government's control over media outlets under Qaddafi led much of the Libyan population to get its news from foreign media sources, such as CNN, BBC, and Al-Jazeera via satellite or to prefer other forms of entertainment, such as watching videos. Libyan television programs offered official government information and existed as propaganda tools. Libyan television is mostly in Arabic, except for a 30-minute news broadcast each evening in English and French. Outside of the occasional sports program offered in English, the majority of Libyan media programming showcases Libya's culture, traditional music, and entertainment.

On January 29, 2006, Qaddafi's son Saif al-Islam Qaddafi announced that the Libyan government would allow private radio and television stations and printed news publications. These new media, Saif claimed, would publish or broadcast uncensored content similar to foreign media outlets such as *Newsweek*, CNN, and *Der Spiegel*. Following this announcement, Saif announced the establishment of a private media company of his own, the One Nine Media, which owned a radio station, Allibya FM, and a multi-million dollar printing house, which was contracted to the German company Heidelberg. One Nine Media was the first privately owned broadcast and printing media outlet in Libya. The resources Saif used to pursue his media projects were invariably the Libyans' own resources, and the intention of his media project was to continue control over radio, television, and print media to ensure these "private" media did not criticize his father. Despite Qaddafi's strict control and censorship of Libyan media, a number of foreign journals, newspapers, radio stations, and television stations were able to broadcast into Libya before Qaddafi's fall from power.

As in other parts of the world, television and radio are extremely popular in Libya, and almost every household has both. Jamahirya Television, the Jamahirya Satellite Television, and the Al Nadi Sports Channel were owned and controlled by the government, and they were used as tools for Qaddafi's propaganda. Private newspapers, some of which are in English, started being printed in Libya in the last decade. For instance, the bi-weekly English language paper, the *Tripoli Post*, is available in print and online throughout the country. In addition, since 2006, foreign newspapers and newsmagazines like *Newsweek* have been imported into the country uncensored. In the years ahead as society becomes increasingly open, so too will the creative spirit, which will release bottled ideas and reveal new directions for expression both within and outside Libya.

NOTES

1. Ali al-Regeie, "Flameless Candles," translated by Ahmed Ibrahim Al-Fagih, quoted in Ahmed Ibrahim Al-Fagih, "The Libyan Short Story" (Ph.D. diss, University of Edinbrugh, 1983).

2. Omar Al-Kikli, "Two Stories: 'Awareness'," *World Literature Today*, Vol. 83, No. 6 (2009), 51.

4

Art and Architecture/Housing

ART

MANY HAVE DESCRIBED LIBYAN ARTS AND ARCHITECTURE as mainly Greco-Roman and Arabic in form and character. Contemporary arts and architecture are visible for everyone to see in Libya today, but no area of life bears the imprint of traditional Libya more gloriously than its arts, housing, and architecture. From the rock art of prehistory in the Sahara to the contemporary paintings blending African, Arab, and European art forms, Libya's artistic legacies span thousands of years. The sheer amount of prehistoric rock art, Roman and Greek ruins, and Italian and Arab art makes Libya one of the most diverse and well-preserved places to see artistic remains in the Mediterranean. The arid conditions of the desert helped preserve the ancient art, which serves as a source of inspiration to visitors, scholars, and contemporary artists.

Rock Art

Libya's rock art is by far the most impressive and extensive in the world, both in quality and sheer numbers. Although still poorly understood, this rock art constitutes a fundamental part of the cultural legacies of the Sahara, especially Libya. A large quantity of rock art is found at Wadi al-Hayat in the Fezzan region.

Rock art comprises drawings of humans; animals such as elephants, buffalo, giraffe, and other animals; plants; and everyday activities painted on, engraved on, or carved from rocks by the earliest inhabitants of the Sahara. In Wadi al-Hayat alone, more than 100,000 engraved rocks and thousands of individual carved images of humans and animals have been found. Possibly dating from about 8,000 years ago, these art works thrived at a time when the Sahara was green with plants and vegetation. Much of the surviving rock art also recorded landscape and climate changes over time in the rocks. Considerable climate changes likely occurred, especially increasing aridity and desertification, and these changes disrupted sedentary agricultural practices during the Garamantian civilization and possibly ushered in pastoralism.

The rock art captured these cultural changes and the effect of climatic variations through symbolism. A nuanced study of the engravings and in-depth analysis of the data can improve our understanding of this significant period of cultural change in the Sahara, especially in refining current understandings of the nexus between the chronological sequence of the art works and linkages between these images, time, and place. For instance, in 2004 and 2005, a group of experts in laser scanning from Bristol University along with government researchers in Libya to scan carved panels. The three-dimensional images were of superior quality and are one of the most complete records of carved rock. Efforts such as this are producing instructive resources for dissemination to locals and to foreign tourists visiting the rock art to help raise consciousness and to stimulate respect for these monuments.

Rock art has also been discovered at Tadrart Acacus on Libya's border with Algeria. In cooperation with the Libyan government, art foundations across the globe have pooled their resources to protect and preserve the artistic legacy of prehistoric Libya. Working together, these organizations have had many sites in Libya designated World Heritage Sites. This designation has rescued these sites so that the world can have a better understanding of Libya's past accomplishments.

Owing to the richness of Libyan rock art, researchers, most notably archaeologists, Egyptologists, and anthropologists, are shifting their attention from Egypt to Libya as an important repository of great and unique prehistoric and primeval arts. Astounding and vibrant images of animals, plants, early pastoralists, ethnic witch doctors, and early artists can be seen on the rocks in the Sahara. Nomadic groups throughout North Africa created art in their travels from modern Libya to Morocco. These magnificent representations survived the vagaries of nature, as an arid desert climate replaced the lush greenery that once dominated the landscape.

Henri Lhote's in the 1950s is often credited with the discovery of Northern Africa's prehistoric arts, but French officers traveling through southern Oran in Algeria in 1847 were the first to report the existence of North African engravings to Europeans. One of the French officers' most distinguishing finds was an animal carving with oxen's horns that were joined together to form a solar disk. The craving was a depiction of a Libyan Sun Goddess. Three years later, the explorer Heinrich Barth, who was crossing the Sahara from Tripoli to Timbuktu, reported similar engravings of animals such as bovid, elephants, ostriches, lions, gazelles, antelopes, and humans in the Fezzan area.

In 1928, Conrad Kilian, the geologist who first informed the world about the huge crude oil reserves in Libya's Sahara, also reported discovering murals depicting a giraffe expedition. Some years later, murals of horse-drawn chariots were also discovered. Lieutenant Brenans, who later became the governor of Tassili, reported the discovery of frescoes in Tassili in 1938. In 1954, an Italian expedition involving Dr. Paradisi, Paolo Grraziose, and Vergara-Caffarelli claimed to have stumbled on a huge deposit of animal engravings and human figures of mostly women in rock shelters in Wadi el Kel, which is about 300 miles south of Tripoli.

It is believed that Lhote learned of these finds and many others and was aware of Brenans's work. After Brenans's death, Lhote decided to carry on with the lieutenant's work by cataloguing the gallery of frescoes in 1956 and 1957. His work led many to erroneously credit him, rather than the French officers traveling in the region in 1847, with the discovery of the rock art of Libya.

Today, the Jamahiriya Museum in Tripoli houses a magnificent collection of ancient relics and treasures, but thousands more can still be found in the Sahara. In Gallery Four of the Jamahiriya Museum stands a Libyan mummy of a child, which is believed to be at least 5,400 years old. In addition, a wholly preserved mummy of a small boy, still in good condition, was found in a place called Wan Muhuggiag. The mummy is evidence that early Libyans had mastered advanced mummification techniques.

The Libyan Sahara has the world's largest collection of prehistoric cave-art sites, featuring a gallery of more than 100,000 prehistoric paintings, drawings, and engravings. Each engraving is unique and tells a story about past generations. One of Lhote's discoveries was a prehistoric painting of a human figure that is about 18 feet tall. For the most part, the Sahara remains the repository of the largest prehistoric paintings in the world.

Dating Libya's many prehistoric paintings, drawings, and engravings has been hampered by enormous problems. While some finds are thought to be more than 12,000 years old, new discoveries push these estimates back to a much earlier period. Archaeological evidence reveals a much lengthier continuity in Libya's deserts. Noting the outdated techniques of dating archaeological finds, some scholars have argued that the first engravings of Libyan ancient arts must have been done between 20,000 and 8,000 BCE. Although the battle over ascertaining the dates of ancient Libyan arts is still raging, scholars agree that some of the finds, such as the prepared-core technique, fishing techniques, hand-axe culture, and red ochre painted faces, must have been in existence for more than 125,000 years. Cultural evidence from Fezzan, the area in which most scholars believe the rock art was produced, reveals that the wall paintings could have been in existence for more than 30,000 years.

Greco-Roman Art

As noted earlier, the Greeks and Romans once invaded and, for a long time, ruled Libya. During these times, the two most prosperous Roman provinces were Tripolitania and Cyrenaica. In fact, they were regarded as parts of the Greco-Roman state, sharing with Libyans not just a common language but also a common national identity and a common legal system. Libyans enjoyed the advantages of urban life like citizens in other Roman cities did. These amenities included the forum, baths, public entertainments, and markets. Many of these legacies are still intact and can be seen in present-day Libya, especially in Leptis Magna. Merchants and artisans came from different parts of the Roman world and for many years established themselves in not only Libya but throughout North Africa. Years after the Romans and Greeks left Libya, the character and forms of Libyan cities reflected their influences; for example, cities in Tripolitania remained distinctly Punic while those in Cyrenaica remained distinctly Greek.

In addition to Libya's indigenous ancient arts, the nation also has some of the best examples of Roman and Greek art in the world. From Leptis Magna to the Temple of Zeus, Libya's elaborate Greco-Roman mosaics, statues, and architecture remain some of the most visible examples of Roman and Greek art anywhere in the world.

Greek and Roman arts are similar, as the Romans borrowed heavily from Greek cultural practices, and both groups incorporated the artistic legacies of cultures they encountered through trade and conquest. Both styles of art provide realistic depictions of human forms, nature, and life in general. The Greeks and Romans prized symmetry and realism in their artistic forms, such as statues, mosaics, paintings, and pottery.

The best example of Greek art remaining in Libya is the amphoras, clay vessels that vary from small-sized, everyday containers to extremely large ones that could be used to transport wine or olive oil. Since amphoras were so common throughout the ancient Greek world, they have been found throughout the Mediterranean and everywhere the Greeks settled in large numbers. Amphoras, like other forms of Greek pottery, were painted or decorated with religious symbols, everyday life events, historical events, or animals.

Two main painting styles are represented on the amphoras. The first utilizes the colors red or black to paint animal or human figures. In the second style, artists dyed the whole piece of pottery black and afterward painted red figures on the darkened pottery. Thousands of pieces of Greek pottery have been found in Libya and are on display in museums throughout the country.

Over the last couple of decades, archaeologists have also discovered large quantities of Roman mosaics and statues in Libya, particularly at Leptis Magna and Cyrene. In the Ancient Roman world, mosaics—a form of art where whole pictures are made up of smaller pieces of material, usually stone or glass—were used in public buildings and private homes to decorate spaces and to tell stories. To make mosaics, artists place small roughly squared pieces of material together to create intricate representations of life and events. One of the best surviving mosaics in the world was found at a villa outside of Leptis Magna in 2000. The "Mosaic of the Gladiators" shows a gladiator crouching next to his fallen victim. In the scene, the victorious gladiator looks exhausted and more relieved than triumphant over his victory. The piece was part of a series of five mosaics that stretched 30 feet and covered the floor of a bath in the villa. Scholars have hailed this mosaic as not only the best preserved mosaic but also one of the more expressive and intricate mosaics found in the Roman world.

The "Mosaic of the Gladiators" may be the most famous mosaic in Libya, but it is certainly not the only one. Hundreds of mosaics have been discovered in not only Leptis Magna but also throughout the country. Their subjects range from representations of animal life, hunts, fishing, and trade to simple nature scenes. Many mosaics have been found in villas and in mansions that were buried under the desert sand after earthquakes. It is possible that many more are still buried in the desert, waiting to be discovered.

In addition to the mosaics, the Romans also left behind a large number of sculptures. Most of these sculptures, like the mosaics, were used to decorate public spaces and homes. However, unlike the mosaics, they were used to honor the wealthy who, for the most part, commissioned these statues. The most common themes expressed by ancient Roman artists dealt with individuals. With the exception of the imperial family, who were represented in ideal and positive ways, artists normally carved realistic statues and took great pains to show all of the flaws and imperfections of their subjects. Also, ancient Roman sculptures, whether located in Libya or in the greater Roman world, included both freestanding statues and reliefs etched into walls, arches, fountains, and other buildings. In Leptis Magna and other Libyan cities, thousands of ancient Roman sculptures can be found etched on many of the buildings as ornamentation.

Early Christian and Byzantine Art

After the conversion of Emperor Constantine, Christianity became the official religion of the great Roman Empire. However, with the fall of the Roman Empire, the Romans and their influence were replaced by the Byzantines, whose influence was felt from Rome throughout the former Roman colonies, including Libya. These complex changes affected Libya from the government to religion to the arts. The artistic legacies of Libya between the fifth and the seventh centuries focused primarily on religious themes.

Libyan artistic works during the period were influenced by Byzantium and dealt with Christian themes. As old Roman temples were turned to Christian churches, gradually and steadily Roman arts gave way to Christian arts. Early Christians used mosaics, as did the Romans, to decorate their places of worship and homes as well as to tell religious stories. Libyan arts, in general, became essentially Christian in outlook and content, and the purpose was largely decorative. In other words, Christian churches were filled with statues and figures representing various biblical figures and, especially in the Coptic and Orthodox churches, saints.

Islamic Art

The decline and fall of the Roman Empire threatened its colonies, including Libya. The once great Roman Empire passed first to the Vandals and later to the Ottomans. The Vandals, like the Romans and Greeks who had ruled ancient Libya, concentrated their attention on the urban areas and largely neglected the outlying areas. At the beginning of the seventh century, the Byzantines completely lost control over North Africa, and the region passed to the Vandals. The Vandals were unable to exert control over the desert Berbers. Berber rebellions became more frequent and, when Muslim invaders arrived, the Vandals provided little or no opposition to the invasion. As a consequence of Arab conquest, new forms of Islamic art emerged. Islamic arts were not necessarily produced for religious purposes but mainly were art forms and styles that were uniquely created in the Islamic world, an area that stretched from Indonesia to the Atlantic coast of Africa.

It cannot be said that Islamic art is strictly Arab and Islamic in form and content. It blends artistic traditions from Greece, Rome, Persia, Africa, India, and Central Asia. These cacophonies of traditions blend to create a separate and unique artistic style that focuses primarily on geometric patterns, bright colors, and calligraphy.

Unlike in European arts, with an emphasis on human figure, Islamic arts, especially religious arts, avoid depicting humans. In Renaissance Europe, like the Americas, artistic representations of Jesus, Mary, God, and other religious figures abound. In Islam, such figures are forbidden, and figures and sculptures of humans, whether religious or secular, are avoided. Islamic art frowns on human representation in artistic works as a way to ward off the possibility of idolatry by worshipping images of religious figures. It is for this reason that no representations of Prophet Muhammad exist in the Islamic world. The uproar that followed the September 2005 *Jyllands-Posten* satirical cartoon of Prophet Mohammad in Denmark was premised on the insulting nature of the cartoon as well as on the injunction against images and representations of the Prophet Muhammad, Muslims, other prophets, and Allah. In all Arabic and Islamic paintings and other forms of representations, even those that deal with the Prophet's life, Muhammad is never painted, sculpted, or visually represented in any way.

Because Islam forbids human subjects in artistic representations, geometric shapes and patterns dominate Islamic art. Geometric patterns are drawn, painted, carved, weaved, or put together on almost any surface. Hence, mosaics of great beauty with intricately designed geometric patterns abound. Patterns are also woven into rugs; etched on mugs, vases, and the like; and painted or drawn on walls, scrolls, papers, domes, and the like.

Calligraphy, another important Islamic art form, is created by using elaborate brush strokes to create beautiful letters. Calligraphy is predominantly used in decorating religious texts such as the Quran and other important documents and to create beautifully decorative scrolls and signs.

Whether in the form of paintings, sculptures, or drawings, Islamic art is created for its sheer beauty. Unlike European and Mediterranean arts that are often commissioned in honor of or to glorify individuals, Islamic art is created to beautify religious texts, places, items, and articles for everyday use. Wealthy and religious-minded individuals do commission artistic works in the Islamic world, but the art is not created to honor them, as Islam forbids this, but to surround them with beauty.

Islamic art in the form of calligraphy, paintings, sculptures, and drawings abounds in great quantity and quality in Libya. With the acceptance of Arabic and Islam as both the official language and official religion of the state, respectively, public and private buildings, documents, and murals in Libya reflect Islamic artistic influences. A walk through Tripoli or any of the other cities in Libya shows this adequately, as government and privately owned establishments display and are decorated with different forms of Islamic art.

Contemporary Art

Qaddafi's 42-year rule had a devastating effect on Libyan arts. Qaddafi's government persecuted writers and artists, forcing many into exile or jail.

Artists, like writers and poets, were locked away in Libyan jails, often without trial, for works the government considered too critical of either Qaddafi or his government. In spite of Qaddafi's repression, Libyan arts did not die out, but they were severely limited, as artists, poets, and writers were forced to work on strictly religious and less politically critical themes. They had to circumscribe their passion and creativity.

Most contemporary Libyan artists have trained in Europe, particularly in Italy. As such, their art often reflects Western themes and styles and portends a danger for indigenous arts because contemporary Libyan artists seldom link indigenous themes and artistic traditions with Western and contemporary traditions. Perhaps the worst impact of Qaddafi's rule on Libyan artistic tradition lies in the country's inability to provide training for local artists. Contemporary Libyan art is, therefore, best described as a troubling hybrid: devoid of a pride in ancestry, it fails to connect with local lore and ethos, and it also has little hope for posterity because of the difficulty inherent in training a corps of local artists to carry on traditional Libyan artistic traditions.

Notwithstanding a lack of local training, Libyan artists have developed a lively art scene, utilizing different media to express themselves. Oil-on-canvass paintings, sculpture, watercolors, sketches, comics, and modern arts display bold colors and geometric shapes, which have become popular staples among Libya's art community. Themes range from traditional life, urban landscapes, and natural landscapes to political issues.

In addition to Qaddafi's dictatorship, another disadvantage contemporary Libyan artists face is the genre's emphasis on the group rather than the individual as a unit of socioeconomic, cultural, and political organization. Artistic works are often regarded merely as the personal expressions of the various artists, not of society's values as a whole. As such, artists were not as severely repressed as writers, and artistic production was not taken over by the government. Qaddafi's government did not target artists as severely as it did the media and publishing, and it did not offer artists much public support. However, Qaddafi's tyranny ensured that contemporary artists such as Abed El MuTalib Hema, Waleed Matar, Abdel Razzag Al Rayani, Basheer Hamooda, and Mar'i El Telesi, among others, concentrated on nonthreatening, nonpolitical, traditional themes. These artists created beautiful works of art, but they were not willing to antagonize the government and risk being jailed or, worse, killed.

As a result, it has been mainly private individuals and artists who have established and sustained museums in Libya. The government has helped establish some museums. One of the primary reasons the government endows selected museums is to protect the numerous rock paintings recovered from Libyan deserts.

Artists unwilling to criticize Qaddafi's government were the norm in Libya, but there were exceptions. For example, Mohammed Zwawi, a cartoonist, attacked political and social problems within Libya, and he remains a classic example of antiestablishment artists in contemporary Libya. One of his cartoons, the "Libyan lyricist . . . and his means of inspiration . . . ," shows a man sweating as he writes at a desk, and the man is surrounded by scenes that seem right out of a horror film. On his desk, a woman with an arrow piercing her heart is set ablaze, a man hangs from the gallows, and another man impaled with a sword is also tied to the gallows. However, a cherub is on the floor, also pierced with an arrow and inside a guillotine. This cartoon demonstrates the danger of producing art in Libya, as you are surrounded by government suppression but cannot outwardly mention it. Zwawi's artwork has both sociocultural and political implications. In other works, Zwawi did not limit his criticism to the Libyan government; he also criticized the United Nations. A number of his works consider the role of oil in world politics, the dominance of the dollar, and other issues facing the Islamic world. It will be interesting to see if the government censorship of the arts will continue as Libyans rebuilds their country.

HOUSING AND ARCHITECTURE

Like its arts, Libya's housing and architectural histories are equally diverse, reflecting influences from the Greeks, Romans, Ottomans, Spaniards, and Italians. Information about the kinds of housing and architecture that existed in ancient Libya can be gleaned only from surviving archeological evidence, especially rock paintings. Millions of years ago, early hominids lived in rudimentary housing like caves, holes, and trees. Early housing systems were predominantly a response to environmental conditions and the need to protect the human body from the elements. Housing and architecture since the Greco-Roman period served not only to provide shelter but to provide beauty.

All over Libya, housing and architecture reflect the various influences of the invaders that have occupied and ruled Libya. From the impressive Roman ruins at Leptis Magna to the Temple of Zeus in Cyrenaica, contemporary Libya boasts of some of the best and most well-preserved examples of ancient Greek and Roman architecture.

Today, the architecture of Tripoli, Benghazi, Fezzan, Bani Waldi, Tobruk, and Cyrene reflects Libya's rich and varied heritage. A walk through these cities to the outskirts reveals Roman and Greek ruins juxtaposed with early Christian churches and Muslim mosques as well as Italian colonial architecture alongside modern skyscrapers and apartment buildings.

The Qaddafi-led revolution of 1968 played a fundamental role in defining and shaping contemporary housing and architecture in Libya. Socialism

The Tripoli skyline seen from a hotel in downtown Tripoli. (AP Photo/Ben Curtis)

inspired Qaddafi's massive housing developments, which were conceived to ensure sufficient accommodations for all Libyans. In 1980, adequate housing was a top priority of the government. Unlike any housing efforts under King Idris, Qaddafi's government undertook the construction of 100,000 housing units, but the project was abandoned soon after it began because it proved too expensive. In 1969, more than 150,000 Libyan families required decent housing, and the housing shortage exceeded 180,000 units. In the 1970s, Qaddafi's massive housing project involved both the government and private sectors. Although later abandoned, the housing sector remained one of the enduring legacies of the late Mohammar Qaddafi.

Today, private and public high-rise apartments are typical in urban areas, but they are relatively recent developments, dating from between 1970 and 1986. The Federal Republic of Germany (then West Germany), France, Turkey, Spain, Italy, the Republic of Korea (now South Korea), and Cuba helped the Libyan government construct 277,500 housing units. However, in 1984, budget allocations for housing fell as government spending dwindled. The suspension and cancellation of many housing contracts by Qaddafi's government led to a shortage in new construction, increased the possibility of overcrowding, and created new slums as Libya's growing population overwhelmed the supply of housing. The remainder of this section will focus on the most elaborate housing and architectural developments in various towns and cities.

Cyrene and Apollonia

Well-preserved ruins of ancient Greek and Roman architecture abound in both Cyrene in Cyrenaica and the port of Apollonia. Cyrene, the most important ancient Greek city in North Africa, boasts a well-preserved mix of Greek and Roman architecture, the most famous of which are the Greek Temple of Apollo, the Temple of Zeus, an amphitheater, and a Roman bath known as Trajan's Bath. A deeply religious people, ancient Greeks dedicated their most important and intricate buildings to the worship of the gods. Despite their pagan religious purposes, some of the temples and public buildings in Cyrene and Apollonia are so impressive that the World Heritage Fund has declared them some of the most important examples of ancient Greek architecture outside of Greece.

Greek architecture, remarkable for its heavy reliance on the use of columns, is usually open on the inside and elaborately decorated with statues, mosaics, and carvings. Temples and buildings such as those for Zeus and Apollo at Cyrene are built in this traditional classical Greek style. They are surrounded on all four sides by massive columns and elaborately decorated with statues, mosaics, and carvings.

The use of columns, the most visible aspect of Greek architecture, was adopted and made popular by the Romans and is widely used in European and American civic buildings today. There are three styles of Greek columns: Doric, Ionic, and Corinthian. Doric columns are relatively plain columns and are easily recognized by their remarkable circle capital or top, which is finished off with a square. Doric columns were most prevalent in the ancient Greek world and were used in the Temple of Zeus.

Ionic columns share similar characteristics with Doric columns, but Ionic columns have scrolls at the capital and are built on a base. Ionic columns are also slightly more decorative than Doric columns. Ionic columns are found throughout Cyrene. The most intricate of the three is the Corinthian. Corinthian columns have intricate carvings of flowers and leaves on the capital and were used in the Temple of Apollo. Because of the significant amount of time that went into making Corinthian columns, they are not as common as Doric and Ionic columns throughout the Greek world. They were, however, the favored style of the Romans.

Unlike churches and mosques, ancient Greek temples were designed to hold or store sacrificial items brought by worshippers rather than be places for worship. Therefore, Greek temples were not built to accommodate large groups of people. However, some temples, such as the Temple of Apollo that was built in the seventh century BCE, were constructed around a natural spring that the ancient Greeks believed had healing properties or holy powers. Large influxes of pilgrims traveled from far and near to reach these temples in their search for healing and wisdom. Thus, the Temple of Apollo, the Trajan Bath, and the Temple of Zeus in Cyrene became some of the most important sites for Greek pilgrims in the ancient world. These ancient buildings are in various states of disrepair in Libya, but the United Nations' World Heritage Fund has declared them World Heritage sites and assumed their maintenance. Work is underway to restore them to their former glory and to raise awareness about them.

Leptis Magna

Leptis Magna, one of the oldest cities in Libya, is 80 miles east of Tripoli, and it is a well-preserved ancient Roman and Carthaginian port city. Originally built by the Phoenicians around seventh century, Leptis Magna was taken over by the Romans after the Punic Wars. The city remains one of the most complete ancient Roman cities in the Mediterranean. The city has been unoccupied since the Arab conquests of the mid-seventh century.

Leptis Magna reached its golden age in the early third century when one of its native sons, Septimius Severus, became a Roman emperor. It must be emphasized that Severus was the first Roman emperor to be born in North Africa, and he made sure that his home city received a revival during his reign. Scholars have noted that Greco-Roman art, housing, and architecture abounded in Libya and North Africa before Severus, but much of the art and architecture was in great disrepair. Severus ensured that these great works were restored and that new ones were constructed during his lifetime. Most writers date the imposing Greco-Roman art and architecture in Libya and North Africa to the time of Severus's rule.

Once emperor, Severus moved to Rome and did not return to Leptis Magna, the city of his birth, until 203. To celebrate his return, the entire city celebrated and honored him by restoring the city's theaters, temples, and other major public works. During his return home, the emperor commissioned the impressive four-sided sculpture "Triumph of Septimius Severus" and a series of colonnaded streets that led to the heart of the city. These, along with Hadrians bath, a well-preserved dock, and an amphitheater, are the key attractions in Leptis Magna today.

As noted earlier, Roman architecture borrowed tremendously from Greek architecture, both in its use of columns and in the design and function of its public and private spaces. However, unlike the Greeks, Romans preferred the use of more decorative Corinthian columns to support their buildings. In Leptis Magna alone, Emperor Severus used over 100 Corinthian columns to

A triumphant arch at Leptis Magnus. (AP Photo/Ben Curtis)

line the main road from the harbor to a renovated square downtown. These columns were designed to impress and dazzle visitors, to reflect the power of Rome, and to display the wealth of Leptis Magna.

In addition to using Corinthian columns almost exclusively, another important innovation developed by Roman architects was using arches and domes in building construction. Contrary to the generally held view that Islamic and Arabic architecture pioneered the use of domes in housing and building construction, the Romans were the first to use these elements. The Romans used arches and domes to create open and airy buildings and monuments. In Leptis Magna, arches and domes abound, and the most important surviving arch in Leptis Magna is the Arch of Septimius Severus. Characteristic of many Roman emperors, Severus commissioned triumphant arches to commemorate their military victories and their accomplishments. The Arch of Septimius Severus in Leptis Magna is one of the most impressive in the entire Roman Empire. This triumphant arch has four sides and is built at the intersection of the two most important roads in the city. It is decorated with intricate carvings and inscriptions and is one the most famous sites in Leptis Magna.

Leptis is also home to a large Roman amphitheater. Historically, Roman theaters were venues for entertainment and sports, thereby providing Romans with an escape from the drudgery of their daily lives. Many Romans spent

The Roman Amphitheater in Leptis Magnus (AP Photo/Ben Curtis)

time in the theaters enjoying and amusing themselves. All large cities throughout the Roman Empire had at least one theater and an arena.

The theater in Leptis Magna overlooks the harbor, and its stage and curved seating area are well preserved. Theaters like the one in Leptis were a venue for plays and gladiatorial games in ancient times. Today, the theater occasionally features public programs.

Roman cities had large aqueducts that carried water from cisterns into the city. Ancient Romans devised innovative plumbing methods to supply water to public and private structures in the city. These aqueducts supplied temples, theaters, and other large public spaces. The water from these aqueducts went to fountains, homes, baths, and toilets. Leptis Magna had a large central bath built in the time of Hadrian. In addition to serving as swimming pools, Roman baths were important gathering places where people bathed and spent time talking and sharing views. The Roman baths solidified community ties.

Islamic Architecture

The term "Islamic architecture" refers to any architecture that is designed and built in the Islamic world and does not necessarily refer only to mosques and other religious buildings. However, the religion of Islam did heavily influence Islamic architecture. The primary builders of Islamic architecture in Libya, as in other North African countries, were the Ottoman Turks.

Since the Ottoman conquests and reign in Libya, the most prevalent styles of housing and architecture in Libya have assumed Arabic and Islamic characteristics. Islamic architecture varies across the Islamic world, but it does have many similar characteristics no matter its locale. Public buildings, such as administrative buildings and mosques, usually have domed roofs. Mosques have between one and four minarets, which are used for calls to prayer as well as for beautification. Within the mosque, there is a small niche called the *mihrabi* that points toward Mecca; to the right of this niche is a *minbar*, or pulpit. In Libya, most mosques are made of white stone, and the only decoration are blue roofs on the dome and minarets. In addition to domes and minarets, Islamic architecture, like Islamic and Arabic art, uses elaborate calligraphy and colors. Attention is paid to beautifying the interior of these buildings, while the exteriors are, more often than not, sparsely decorated.

Similarly, in other public buildings, the interiors are far more important than the exteriors, and traditional buildings in Libya are usually plain on the outside. However, the interiors are elaborately decorated with geometric and calligraphic designs, which make them appealing and welcoming.

Across the Islamic world, perhaps the major variation in Islamic and Arabic housing and architecture can be found in the materials used in building construction. In Libya, housing and other buildings must contend with extreme temperatures, especially in the desert regions. Builders and architects take this into consideration when they design and build. The types of materials used generally are those that absorb heat, and the colors are usually light to reflect rather than absorb heat. For the most part, buildings are painted in light khaki or brown colors, and building materials are traditionally made out of mud and straw bricks.

One important aspect of Islamic architecture is the delineation of public from private spaces. Buildings in Libya, as throughout the Muslim world, are divided into public and private spaces. Private spaces are reserved exclusively for family members and close friends. The demarcation between public and private spaces is not limited to private dwellings alone but is reflected in public buildings such as government offices.

Colonial Italian Architecture

The Italian occupation of Libya in the first half of the twentieth century also left an indelible mark on the landscape of Libya's major cities. In Tripoli, for example, Italian colonial buildings sit alongside ancient Greco-Roman ruins, mosques, and contemporary structures. During the reign of Mussolini, Italian architecture in Libya was designed not just for functionality but also to impress. Fascist Italy wanted its colonial architecture to show the power of modern Italy and, therefore, reflected a blend of classic Roman architecture and new, modern architecture comprised of marble and granite. Like their Greco-Roman forbearers, Italian structures in Libya also have towering and well-decorated columns.

Ghadame

Ghadame is one of Libya's most unique and oldest cities. It lies deep in the Sahara desert and was founded sometime around the first century BCE. Ghadame is one of the oldest continuously inhabited cities in Africa. Less than 10,000 people live in the city today. Despite its sparse population, Ghadame is a major tourist attraction in contemporary Libya.

The city was originally built along the trans-Saharan trade routes and flourished until the fifteenth century when the Atlantic became the most important route. Details of the sociopolitical structures of this ancient city are lost. Numerous cave and rock paintings reveal glimpses of the old city. The city is composed of two parts today. One part is the old city, which has remained almost unchanged for hundreds of years; it is still used during in the summer months. The buildings in the old city are designed to ward off the extreme heat of the Libyan summers and are more efficient in doing this than are the modern buildings in the new city. Much of the architecture was built using straw and mud bricks, and, like most Islamic architecture, the outsides of the buildings are plain. The orange walls and buildings of the old city are topped by white paint that reflects the sun and helps to maintain cooler temperatures inside. A typical house in Ghadame has at least three floors. The first floor is used to store goods, the second floor is used as living spaces, and the rooms on roof are reserved for women.

The most distinguishing feature of the entire city is the network of tunnels and alleyways. Ghadame is laid out so that every building is attached to the one next to it, and people can travel throughout large portions of the city without ever stepping foot in the harsh desert sunlight. It is one of the best examples in the world of how humans have adapted to a harsh climate. In 1986, the city has been designated a World Heritage Site.

The new city, on the other hand, is built completely according to European or American standards, which do not suit the local climatic conditions. Thus, buildings in Ghadame reflect two different styles, and the old and new cities belong to two radically separate times. A comfortable and enjoyable environment can be achieved in Libya's desert region if appropriate and effective systems are devised to incorporate the old into the new housing structures.

Contemporary Architecture

As noted earlier, contemporary Libya architecture is a blend of desert, Roman, Greek, Islamic, Spanish, and Italian architecture. Contemporary architects reflect these multiple layers of heritages. Today, Libya has skyscrapers and modern buildings similar to those found in the United States, but with a Libyan twist.

5

Cuisine and Traditional Dress

INTRODUCTION

LIBYA, A RELATIVELY NEW STATE, is situated in a land that has been conquered, occupied, and administered by outsiders for centuries. The Phoenicians, who originally established trading posts in Libya, were the first invaders to settle and rule Libya. They were followed by the ancient Greeks, Romans, Spaniards, Ottomans, and later the Italians before Libya became independent in 1951 after a few years under the United Nations' watch. All of these foreigners not only ruled Libya but also left their imprints on Libyan cuisine and traditional dress. This is not to say that Libyans did not possess their own cuisines and sartorial traditions prior to the arrival of these outsiders, but the cuisines and sartorial traditions of Libya before contact with outsiders may have been lost or adapted to those imposed by the outsiders. Much of what is eaten and worn in contemporary Libya can be traced to the influences of these outsiders.

CUISINE

The influences of the various peoples that have ruled Libya can be found in Libya's architecture, languages, and sartorial tradition, and cuisine. The nature and topography of Libya's land has had a greater influence on and fundamental role in its food culture. As noted earlier, Libya faces the

Mediterranean Sea to the north and Egypt to the east. On the southeast is Sudan, while Chad and Niger are to the south. Algeria and Tunisia are to the west. With the exception of the north, Libya is bounded by arid desert with little or no surface water to allow for any meaningful cultivation. With few or no major rivers, food cultivation is limited to the north where, the land is watered by the rains that fall on the Mediterranean coast. In other areas, underground water systems, especially to the east, west, and south, allow for marginal cultivation. Libya's geography, like many of its neighbors in the Maghreb, greatly impacts the type of food available and enjoyed. Libya's location at the fringes of the Mediterranean coastal belt and in the desert regions of North Africa has led to a diverse culinary culture.

Contemporary Libyan cuisines are a blend of Arab, Mediterranean, and North African dishes. The types of food eaten in Libya vary based on the region of the country, for example, the types of food available deep in the Sahara differ from those of the coast. However, the majority of Libyans serve and cook meals in traditional ways. The major cities are filled with fast food stands and restaurants; most are franchise shops from different parts of the world. Rural dwellers eat at home, except occasionally when they find themselves in the cities. Labor migrants, tourists, and educated Libyan urban dwellers, mostly youths, patronize restaurants. The average Libyan frequents restaurants only on special occasions such as Valentine's Day, religious ceremonies of all kinds, birthdays, or when traveling from one place to another.

Although outsiders who ruled Libya over the last 1,500 years have left a strong impact on the food produced and consumed in the country, food remains one of the most enduring cultural practices and is both deeply personal and communal. The way food is prepared, served, and consumed has deep cultural meanings. Ingredients used in preparing foods also have cultural meanings; certain foods are served only at specific rituals, religious ceremonies, or occasions. A region's cuisine offers invaluable insights into both its daily life and values.

Contemporary Libyan food can be traced to the days of the Roman Empire when North Africa was considered the breadbasket of Rome. Thousands of Roman farmers came to North Africa to cultivate the fertile coastal belt and river regions, and they sent the produce back to Rome. The primary crop in Roman Libya was grains, and grains were used in making bread, beer, and other food stuffs. The Arab invasions of the eighth century brought many new recipes and spices from as far away as China, which greatly expanded and enriched the Libyans' diet. The Ottoman occupation brought a new way of cooking meats that can best be described as barbequing. Italy's occupation also left a lasting legacy on Libyan food by introducing pastas, a modern-day staple in Libya. Libyan food has slowly transitioned over the

Two Libyan fishermen prepare a fishing boat in the harbor of the city of Sabrata, Libya. (AP Photo/Abdel Magid Al Fergany)

centuries into a simple but hearty collection of recipes with influences from Europe, Africa, and Asia. Libya, like most of North Africa, owes its food heritage to all of the people who have called Libya home, each leaving a distinct mark on the nation.

Islam and Food

Islam, like Judaism, has dietary laws that its adherents must follow. Islamic dietary laws divide food into two types: *halal* and *haram*. The first is clean, holy, and acceptable, and the other is considered filthy, unholy, and unacceptable to Islam. Muslims are allowed to eat any food that is *halal* and are forbidden to eat any food that is *haram*. Under certain circumstances, *halal* can become *haram* and *haram* can become *halal*. Only on the pain of death can Muslims eat *haram*. Under such conditions, Muslims are expected to use their discretion to save their lives.

Forbidden and unforbidden foods are too numerous to list. The determinant of which food is forbidden and which is not deals largely with cleanliness, both in secular and spiritual conceptualizations. Foods that are forbidden in Islam include dogs, pigs, and any product thereof; gelatin from any animal that is not *halal*; meats obtained from animals that are not slaughtered in a manner prescribed by Islam; meats obtained from animals that are *halal* but dead and not slaughtered; anything containing alcohol; blood; anything from a human; all carnivores or birds of prey; and any non-*halal* additives.

Halal food can become *haram* if subjected to conditions that turn it to *haram*. For instance, Islam has specific requirements for slaughtering animals; hence, any animal that is killed without observing the requirements easily becomes *haram*. The required way to slaughter animals under Islamic law is called *dhabiha*. This method requires that the person doing the slaughtering must, first of all, pray over the animals. Then he must use a sharp knife that can cut the carotid artery, throat, windpipe, and jugular vein of the animal simultaneously and in such a quick motion that the animal will not suffer pain. The spinal cord must not be broken and must remain attached to the animal's body. The goal is to quickly cut off the blood and oxygen supply to the animal so that it dies without suffering. With the exception of fish and other seafood, all *halal* animals must be killed in this way.

In addition to the previously mentioned conditions, *halal* food can become *haram* if a dog or a pig touches it. Such food must be thrown away. As for individuals, Islam requires thorough washing or bathing if someone touches a *haram* food. In Libya, as in all Islamic countries of the world, *halal* items are carried in grocery stores and prepared in restaurants.

Importance of Meals

Meals are an important part of family life in Libya. In fact, meals afford families the opportunity to gather and reflect on the day's activities and to share individuals' experiences with other members of the family. Most Libyan families eat at home and go to restaurants only on Fridays and on special occasions, if they go at all. This practice keeps the family together and makes it strong.

According to cultural traditions, women eat after men, and meals are prepared and served by women. Men and women eat separately in Libya. Unlike in countries of northern Europe and the United States, lunch is the most important meal of the day in Libya; hence, families and friends gather together to enjoy a hearty lunch. Except during Ramadan, Libyans do not eat before the sun rises or after it sets.

Common Foods

Globalization and industrialization continue to open Libya, like the rest of Africa, to food cultures from different parts of the world. Rice, beans, pasta, and the like abound in Libya just as they do in other parts of the world. However, the four most common and important staples in Libyan food culture are olives, grains, dates, and milk. These four staples are taken whole and in processed forms. Olives, grains, dates, and milk are processed, for instance,

A boy cleans up after lunch in a traditionally decorated home in the ancient town of Ghadames. (AP Photo/John Moore)

into cheese and yogurt, olive oil, bread, sauces, and candies. Although some grains consumed by Libyans can also be brewed into beer, beer and alcohol are illegal in Libya. These four staples—olives, grains, dates, and milk—are the backbone of the Libyan diet.

Traditionally, Libyans supplement bread and other grain products with fresh ingredients such as fresh and dried raisins, cooked syrups or sauces, and vegetables. As in much of the Mediterranean world, olive oil is used in almost every facet of Libyan cooking. Libyans use olive oil, particularly extra virgin olive oil, in making breads, pastas, couscous, and many other dishes. Virgin and extra virgin olive oil are produced by extracting oil from olives using cold pressing techniques; the higher the quality of the olive, the better olive oil obtained.

Popular Dishes

As noted previously, globalization and industrialization have opened Libya to food cultures from other parts of the world. Rice, beans, pasta, and the like abound in Libya, and different kinds of bread are available everywhere in Libya. Popular dishes include lebrak, couscous, mb'atten, pastas, and seafood.

Utshu, which is also called a'eish or bazin, has grain as its base, which is the case for most Libyan foods. Utshu is probably a Neolithic dish and is a

Libyans shopping at a vegetable market in Benghazi. (AP Photo/Hussein Malla)

traditional Libyan food that is made from dough and eaten with sauce. Utshu is one of the mainstays of the Libyan diet and one of the most popular dishes in the country. To make utshu, the dough is kneaded into semispherical balls that are placed in the middle of a large bowl, and sauce is poured around them. Utshu is a solid, thick food and requires a great deal of energy to prepare. Women sit for a long time, often on the bare floor, bending over the hot pan. They wrap the pan in a thick cloth that they hold with their feet as they turn the wooden ladle (locally called *aghenjay*) with both hands and mix the dough with enormous strength. Because of the effort required, most women prefer using machine-made wheat flour than traditionally prepared flour, which is usually tougher. The sauce prepared with utshu also deserves a special mention. In most homes, meat and vegetables are fried with chili powder, onions, turmeric, garlic, tomato puree, and salt then mixed with either minced lamb or beef. The mixture is then cooked until almost done, and potatoes and pumpkin are added. Once cooked through, the sauce is poured around the dough, and the dish is served while hot. Depending on the type of sauce used, utshu can be eaten for breakfast, lunch, or dinner.

Z'ummeeta or zumita is another dough-based dish prepared by mixing flour with water. Once the dough is mixed with water, the paste is kneaded until it becomes firm and doughy. Z'ummeeta is eaten with olive oil and chili sauce. It takes only few minutes to prepare z'ummeeta, and it is, therefore, usually eaten as breakfast or whenever there is a need for some kind of fast food.

Couscous, or kesksoo, is perhaps one of the most popular foods not just in Libya but across North Africa. It can be made either from wheat or barley. Whichever is preferred, the wheat or barley is ground into coarse flour and then boiled. Couscous is typically eaten with a vegetable and meat sauce. Couscous is also popular in Europe, an eloquent testimony of its popularity throughout the Mediterranean.

Unlike utshu, z'ummeeta, and couscous, mb'atten is a Libyan specialty food. Mb'atten is usually prepared for special occasions, celebrations, or festivities. It is made by cutting potatoes lengthwise into small, thin slices. The slices are kept in pairs, and each pair is about three millimeters in thickness. The slices are connected at the base to form a sandwich. The potato sandwich is then stuffed with minced meat, either beef or lamb, and herbs before it is fried.

Shorba is Libyan soup. It is made by frying a freshly cut large onion along with garlic in clarified butter, called ghee, until both turn golden brown. Pieces of meat, usually lamb or beef, are added with turmeric, tomato puree, salt, chili, and other spices. The mixture is then seasoned with curry powder, sugar, and water. The soup is simmered until the meat is done. Other ingredients usually added include cooked chickpeas, garlic, olive oil, and lemon. The soup is eaten with warm bread.

Lebrak, another Libyan dish, is made from a variety of leaves; vine leaves are used most often. Vine leaves, rice, tomato, herbs, garlic, and spices are mixed with meat, usually beef or lamb, and rice and then wrapped and rolled up with leaves around it. The wrapped packages are placed on top of a few loose leaves in a pot to prevent the lebrak from burning. A smaller lid is then placed on the pot to add pressure on the leaves and prevent them from opening up. A small quantity of water is added, and the pot is gradually heated up for about 30 minutes until the rice is cooked thoroughly. The cooked lebrak is served with olive oil.

Of all the many outsiders that ruled Libya, Italy had one of the biggest influences on Libyan cuisine. Today pasta is an important part of Libya's culinary culture. Macaroni, small, curved, hollow pasta often served with tomato sauces, is popular and eaten throughout Libya. In Italy, pasta and sauce are prepared in separate pans, but in Libya, the pasta and sauce are boiled together.

Ironically, although Libya is on the Mediterranean Sea, seafood is not eaten often. One major reason is that Libya has few natural protected harbors, which greatly impairs its ability to exploit the vast coastline. Seafood is served

A man shopping in a fish market in Benghazi. (AP Photo/Sergey Ponomarev)

mostly in Tripoli. Modern fishing techniques and the construction of new harbors have led to the increased appearance of seafood outside of Tripoli.

Traditional Cooking Methods

The sand oven is a traditional Tuareg method of cooking bread; freshly prepared dough is buried under the hot sand. Extreme desert temperatures ensure that sand ovens are as, and usually more, effective than conventional ovens. In the summer, Libya gets so hot that walking barefoot on the sand is comparable to walking on embers. Traditional Libyans have taken advantage of the extreme heat from the sun to bake, among other things, bread, potatoes, and eggs by burying them under the sand for a short time. In some conditions, fire is added to speed the process as a type of instant baking. In the case of dough buried in the sand, a couple of whacks and a good shake clean the bread, and then it is ready to be eaten. The use of sand ovens is limited to Tuaregs living in the deserts. Libyans living in the major cities and coastal areas now use modern stoves and electric ovens.

BEVERAGES

Alcoholic drinks and beer are banned in Libya in accordance with Islamic law, but locally brewed beer and other alcoholic drinks can be bought illegally. The quality of locally brewed beer and alcohol is doubtful. Bottled mineral water and different kinds of soft drinks are readily available and are consumed everywhere in the country. Libyans drink a lot of fruit juices; the most popular is orange juice. Oranges can be bought from street stalls when the fruit is in season.

Libyans drink a lot of tea, which is often thick and served in small glasses. American or British coffee, which is collectively called Nescafe, is also available in Libya. In the most traditional homes, beverages are not served before meals.

Tea drinking is one of the most significant social occasions in Libya. Tea drinking is a time when family members get together daily to laugh, chat, and discuss various events and life in general. Libyan tea can be a syrupy black or green tea and is usually served very strong and thick. Unless using American or British tea, traditional Libyan tea is prepared by steaming water in a teapot and adding a handful of green or black tea leaves. The mixture is left to boil for a long time. The pot is then removed from the heat, cubes of sugar are added, and the pot is returned to the stove to boil for a few more minutes. When the tea is ready, it is left to settle and then served in small glasses.

In traditional Libyan society, once the tea is done, it is first poured into a mug; an empty mug is kept aside for use in cooling down the hot tea. The process is as follows: the contents of the first mug are poured into the empty mug until the second mug is almost filled. The second mug is then raised, and its contents are poured into the almost empty mug. This is done continuously not less than 20 or 30 times. In the process of continuously pouring the hot tea back and forth between the two mugs, a froth or foam that Libyans call *reghwet* or *reghwa* is produced. The foam is then poured into smaller glasses and served to family members. To produce this froth, the mug with the tea must be raised by stretching the arm over the head as high as possible while the tea is being poured into the other mug. The process is then repeated by lowering the raised hand while raising the other one until enough froth has been produced. This process is especially done on special occasions.

Tea is served in rounds, and at the end of the third round, roasted peanuts or roasted almonds are served. After the last cup has been drunk, a vessel called a *guerba*, which contains milk or spring water, is passed around. The person drinking must not breathe into the vessel and must remove the vessel from his or her lips before breathing again. Tea is served after meals in Libya, unlike in the United States and Great Britain. Green tea is useful to the body as it aids digestion and also helps aide digestion, especially after a heavy meal.

Fasting

Fasting is an important part of Libyan life. It is an important part of worship in Islam, and almost all Libyans are Muslim. Islam requires that all

Muslims observe the fast during Ramadan, the holy month, which commemorates the celebration of when the Holy Quran was revealed to Prophet Muhammad. For Muslims, fasting is considered a sacred time for religious reflection when adherents turn away from their material needs, like food, in total submission to Allah. During this month, Muslims are forbidden from consuming anything except water between daybreak and sunset. Only children, pregnant and nursing women, and those who are physically or mentally unfit are exempt from this religious obligation. Large meals are served before the sun rises and after it sets.

Traditional Dress

As in all human communities, sartorial traditions are factors of geography and culture. Irrespective of time and epoch, Libya's extreme climate warrants that its inhabitants wear such dress as can keep them safe from the heat of the sun. Particularly in southern Libya, where the sun shines almost all the days of the year, Libyans dress sparingly in loose cotton shirts worn with trousers and a cloak for men and on full-length robes for women. Men usually complete their dress with a flat, brimless cap, while women cover their heads with either shawls or *hijabs*. Traditional Libyan clothing is usually long, loose fitting, and made of lightweight cotton materials.

Both men and women in traditional Libyan households wear clothes in natural colors such as brown and tan. The primary function of clothing is to protect the wearer from the intense sun, so most of the body is covered. Most Libyans live in the cities, and there are both traditional and Western clothes. Older men and women continue to dress in more traditional clothing, especially during festivals and celebrations. Traditional clothing for men is a white, long gown that is worn over a shirt and a pair of trousers. More often than not, most men wear white or black hats. Most women's gowns cover both their bodies and heads in keeping with Islamic tradition. It is common to see members of the same family dressed in both traditional and in western styles. Young men and women in urban areas primarily wear modern clothing. Urban women wear bright-colored dresses as well as jeans and tee-shirts like urban men.

The coastal regions of Libya share a similar climate with other Mediterranean regions and have cool temperatures but bright sunshine. In these areas, the cloth used for clothing is usually thick to keep in the heat. In the Sahara, temperatures can range from very cold during the night to extreme heat during the day, so Libyan clothing must be able to protect its wearers from both the sun during the day and also from the cold temperatures during the night.

Tuareg tribesman pause after dancing for tourists in al-Ramla on the northern edge of the Sahara desert in western Libya in 2004. Since the government of Muammar Qaddafi began its campaign to open its doors to the outside world, tourists are increasingly visiting Libya. (AP Photo/John Moore)

Western Impact

Today in Libya, people mix various forms of dress to create their own style. Young people, in particular, are more inclined to challenge the traditional dress and embrace Western dress. Most young people in Libya wear tee shirts and jeans, and young women often add veils to conform to Islamic expectations. Businessmen and government officials throughout Libya wear suits and seldom wear the flowing gowns that are traditionally worn in Libya.

6

Gender Roles, Marriage, and Family

FAMILY

IN LIBYA, LIKE IN OTHER PARTS OF AFRICA, the family is the basic unit of sociocultural, economic, and political control. The father, as the head of the family, makes decisions for and on the behalf of the entire family. Other members of the family defer to him both in private and public matters. Customarily, the younger family members—females and males—must not only obey him but also not defy his authority in private or in public. As in other patriarchal societies, inheritance is passed down through the male line.

In precolonial Libya, households were comprised of both married and unmarried children of the head of the family. Together with the family head, married and unmarried sons along with their respective families lived in the same house. After the female children married, they moved out of their fathers' houses to join their husbands' households, but they kept their fathers' last names. Just because a young woman married into her husband's family did not mean that she, in a practical sense, had left her father's family to join another family. She remained a member of her father's family, and she could, in case of divorce, return to her father's house at any time. Libyan families were, not surprisingly, large in size.

When the head of the family died, his sons were expected to perpetuate the process by creating their own large families. Because of the primary importance placed on large families and as in most traditional African societies, male children were prized more than females. Libyans impressed on female children that they were inferior to males and that females must cater to males. Male children were brought up to demand concern and care from women. Females, irrespective of age, status, and education, were regarded as creatures set apart by God (Allah) to be weaker in mind, soul, and body than men. Unlike men, women were considered less disciplined but more sensual than men. As such, they were constantly in need of protection from not just the excesses of other men but also from their own impulses. However, since families are enlarged through marriage, it was expected that all Libyans—males and females—marry and have children, an expectation most especially of males, to perpetuate the family.

In contemporary times, industrialization and globalization have spurred labor migration, and the movement of men and merchandise from rural to urban areas. Hence, many young people, most especially males, have moved away from rural areas, and from their traditional homes, to find work in the cities, where they eventually begin their own families outside of their fathers' household. While this migration has impacted the family structure tremendously, it does not diminish the power of the family. The chances for a young man to find employment in business, education, or government depend largely on his family connections. Consequently, regardless of whether a young man stays in the rural area with his father or migrates into the city, the family connection is an essential asset he cannot afford to lose. Networks of relationships, especially family connections, serve as a key component of Libyan public life.

Marriage

In Libya, marriage, the cornerstone of the family, is the bedrock of the society. As in many parts of Africa, marriage is not just a union between a man and a woman, but a relationship between families, clans, and, as the case may be, communities. In precolonial Libya, traditional marriages usually took place within the family as people usually married their first cousins. The practice was for oldest sons to marry their uncles' oldest daughters. Since marriage is seen as the joining together of two families, it was believed that by marrying within the extended family, marriage would strengthen family ties. As a result, forced marriages were common as parents sought to strengthen family ties by forcing their children and wards to marry spouses the parents chose.

Although the practice was generally accepted in precolonial Libya, contemporary Libyans frown upon forced marriage and marriage within the extended family, particularly in the urban areas. Rural society, on the other hand, has been slower to change and has insisted on preserving the tradition.

A Libyan woman has her face painted in the colors of the former royal flag during a demonstration against Libyan leader Muammar Qaddafi in Benghazi. (AP Photo/ Kevin Frayer)

Since the One September Revolution, the military coup that brought Muammar Qaddafi to power, forced marriages have been outlawed, and the legal dignity and equality of women, especially their right to choose their husbands, has been enshrined in the nation's constitution. Notwithstanding these changes, the desire for children to marry someone with close family ties still persists.

From the colonial period to the contemporary period, marriage has been considered the primary goal of every Libyan. Women, for the most part, usually get married in their early twenties, while men are expected to get married in their thirties. Difficult economic problems resulting from the collapse of the oil trade and economic recession of the 1980s have increased the tendency to delay marriage, and many men are not financially able to get married until they are in their mid-thirties and forties. Men are expected to be economically established and to have enough money to pay the bride price, which varies from family to family and increases based on how desirable the bride's family is.

Whether forced or not, once a marriage is consummated, the husband is considered the head of the household. He reserves the right to make decisions for his wife and children. Although the Qaddafi government tried to implement equal rights for women, these efforts were relatively unsuccessful in changing gender roles in marriage. Women, no matter how educated or wealthy, are still subservient to their husbands, and this is particularly true in rural Libyan societies.

Marriage in Libya is between one man and one woman. This has implications for types of marriage allowed in contemporary Libya. As in most African societies, gay, lesbian, and transsexual practices are considered aberrant behaviors and are, therefore, frowned upon. If these practices do exist, they are carefully kept away from the public.

Like any typical Muslim community, Libya allows polygamy, a system of marriage that allows for more than one wife for men. However, under Libyan laws, a man is allowed to take a second, third, or fourth wife only if he obtains the consent of his first wife. The law is, however, silent on the procedure for obtaining this consent. Even after consent is obtained, and without regard to how it is procured, the man must demonstrate that he is able to support all of the wives. Monogamy is on the ascent in most parts of Libya as legal restrictions combined with harsh economic conditions force most men to adopt monogamous lifestyles. In addition, educated and economically independent females are more likely to desire a monogamous marriage and to do away with traditional values.

Besides the training of their daughters for their future role as a wife and mother, families consider it an honor for their daughters to be virgins before marriage. In fact, a woman's virginity is considered a thing of joy not just for her but also for her family. Men consider their honor irreparably damaged if their daughters or other women in the family conduct themselves in ways considered irresponsible. Daughters, sisters, wives, and mothers are expected to be virtuous, above reproach, prudent, decorous, and shy. Irresponsible behaviors, especially in the public, could destroy a family's reputation and honor with little hope of repair. Premarital sex is discouraged. Female virginity before marriage and sexual fidelity after marriage are considered essentials to maintaining a family's honor. The discovery of any transgression or irresponsible behavior traditionally compels males in a family to punish any offending woman, irrespective of age, status, or education.

To prevent loss of virginity and the associated dishonor and shame, most families marry off their daughters earlier than necessary. In fact, most families prefer to and enthusiastically marry off their daughters at the earliest possible age as a measure to preserve family honor and social prestige. After the marriage ceremony, it is customary for the young bride to go to her bridegroom's family home. There, she will live the rest of her life under the constant watch, and sometimes extremely critical and often intrusive nature, of her mother-in-law. More often than not, such critical monitoring by mothers-in-law has led to a great deal of friction within the family, including between husbands and wives.

Much has changed since 1969, but traditional Libyan society still places a higher premium on male children than on the female children. Unless a woman bears male children, the groom's family, and of course society, will not accord her any respect, status, or dignity.

Divorce

Libyan secular law and Islamic law allow for divorce, but the practice is frowned upon socially. Compared to the United States, the rate of divorce in Libya is extremely low. It is important to stress that, unlike in the United States, Libya does not recognize anything that resembles a no-fault divorce. To obtain a divorce in Libya, a party must show cause. The costs of obtaining a divorce in Libya may account for the infrequency of divorce in Libya compared to the United States. Also, divorce is viewed negatively in Libya and is less common than in other parts of the world. However, once a divorce occurs in Libya, the woman usually moves back into her father's home; a woman's ability to live on her own is limited by the conservative culture of Libya.

Motherhood

Like in other parts of Africa, many young girls in Libya looks forward to the day when they will get married and raise a family of their own. Motherhood, therefore, is seen as the most important, God-given role of a woman. Qaddafi detailed in his *The Green Book* the general perception of women in contemporary Libya. In Libya, women and men are equal under the law, but they are biologically and naturally different. Therefore, they have different roles and spheres of influence in the society. The most important aspect of any woman's life is to be a mother. Anything that takes a woman away from her role of parenting and motherhood is, according to *The Green Book*, a form of "coercion and dictatorship."[1] Accordingly, a woman's primary function, no matter her status, education, and class, is to reproduce and propagate both the society and the species. While women should be considered equals, they are not treated equally with men. A woman's ability to become pregnant and bear children makes her unsuitable for many types of work outside of the home, especially if such work infringes on her ability to be a mother.

In addition, women are considered caregivers, especially since they give birth to children in the first place. Every Libyan expects that a mother will take care of her offspring and as a result, daycare centers are rare in Libya. As earlier noted, because of the premium placed on male children, a woman earns respect, dignity, and love from her husband and from her entire family when she has male children. For this reason, most Libyan women prefer male children, and it is not uncommon to find strong bonds of unity between mothers and their sons. The Quran and *The Green Book* prescribe breast-feeding exclusively, although it is common in urban areas for women to switch between breastfeeding and bottle feeding their young children. This combination allows women the freedom to participate in workplace activities sooner than those who exclusively breastfeeding. Also families, especially in the urban centers, who can afford the services of nannies employ them in caring for their children.

The roles and status of women in Libyan society since 1969 has elicited considerable debates. On the one hand, many argue that the Qaddafi regime's efforts at female emancipation were premised on the need to provide an important source of employment for an economy that was constantly in need of workers. On the other hand, others argue that his government was merely concerned with enlarging its political support. Championing women's rights was the Qaddafi's government's way of currying favor and ensuring women's support. However, one curious fact about women's emancipation in Libya is that the government's efforts were constrained by Islamic tenants related to gender roles, which could have accounted for its slow pace.

Since the 1980s, relationships between the sexes and within families have witnessed tremendous changes, especially as global trade and mass media have succeeded in popularizing new ideas, and new practices. Labor migrants arrived in the country with new thoughts and values that were radically divergent from those of traditional Libyan societies. These circumstances, combined with legal requirements, have altered Libya's perceptions of women and all facets of life. Traditional perceptions of kinship ties, family connections, and relationships with ancestral communities, especially in the rural areas, have undergone change.

New vistas in employment, particularly in the oil industry, have created spaces for women and increased their upward social mobility and economic progress. In recent decades, many women were homebound and illiterate, but they are now more often educated and employed in positions traditionally reserved for men. This development has led to a sense of individualism among Libyan women. These educated young people favor marrying partners they choose for themselves and setting up their own households rather than living with their parents. In addition, they prefer monogamy to polygamy. The introduction of adult education, social security, free medical care, and other government policies and programs has diminished the need for the elderly rely on their children. This is often the case for elderly living in both traditional areas and in the cities.

Unlike most African societies, traditional Bedouin women are freer than their urban counterparts. In traditional Libyan society, Bedouin women, for the most part, do not wear the veil; they consider it a symbol of inferiority and seclusion. They play important roles as farmers, herders, mothers, and caregivers in tribal life. Their relative independence did not generally license exposure to strangers, but women in rural villages are able to actively participate in the affairs of their communities, usually as farmhands and laborers. The same is seldom true of their urban counterparts.

Although urban women are educated, cultured, and socially aware, they tend to be less adventurous in social relations and in the sartorial tradition. Among upper-class families in urban areas, women play little or no economic roles. Their responsibilities are limited to procreation and caring for the household. Invariably, a much greater separation of the sexes is enforced in the cities than in the rural areas because farm work and village life make sexual separation almost impossible.

The Impact of Urbanization on Women

From the Hellenistic period to contemporary times, Libyans have resided in cities, most especially in Tripoli, Benghazi, Misurata, and a few other cities. Migratory processes and urbanization have operated in Libya over a considerable length of time. Urbanization had a profound impact on ancient Libyan culture and continues to impact contemporary Libyan culture. Libyan cities have evolved into crucibles of social change. For instance, cities were marginal to the development of the Sanusi brotherhood because it drew followers from the rural tribal communities in the desert. However, in more recent times, more Libyans see the cities as major centers of fascination, and the cities draw more people out of their rural villages or communities. Familial ties dissolve and old rules are broken as young, educated Libyans find their places in the world. The Sanusi and many of the other brotherhoods have, therefore, moved into the cities.

Rural to urban migration effectively began during Italian colonization and led to the influx of large numbers of workers to the cities. These workers sought not only economic opportunity but also a wider range of sociocultural, recreational, and educational experiences. The population densities of major cities created an atmosphere that allowed for more mixing among the sexes. However, increasing urbanization came with a price: housing shortages. As the available housing became saturated with immigrants, old family houses became tenements. An offshoot of this development was the growth of squatter communities or slums that provide accommodation for those who cannot get accommodation in the city centers.

The hustle and bustle of cities also creates more opportunities for those of the opposite sex to intermix socially. While it is still frowned upon for an unmarried couple to be seen in public together, the anonymity of the major cities allows couples to go out in public without escorts. Dating has flourished in Libya since the colonial period, but it was done under the supervision of the couple's families. Life in the cities now affords youths opportunities to date outside of their family's control.

In contemporary Libya, urbanization has impacted the division of labor. Urban women have jobs outside of their homes, and women have played fundamental roles as teachers, nurses, pilots, and even Qaddafi's personal bodyguards. Working outside the home is not common in rural Libya.

Since the 1970s, the government has opened up spaces for women to participate in public life. For example, between 1976 and 1980, Libya's Development Plan required employment opportunities for a larger number of women "in those spheres which are suitable for female labor," although the identification of what constitutes work "suitable for women" is determined by Libyan tradition.

In real terms, the emancipation of women has taken different forms. Since the 1970s, urban women between the ages of 35 and 45 are more likely to wear western-style clothes, while those older than 45 are more likely to wear the veil and observe other customary dress codes. Today, women are taking employment opportunities in government and in private industry. The majority of women now drive cars and travel without their husbands, other male companions, or other women companions. They are also seen more often in public places like shopping malls.

Beginning in 1970, the Qaddafi-led revolutionary government enacted laws aimed at regulating female employment. In addition, these laws ensured equal pay for equal qualifications and equal work opportunities regardless of sex. Equal pay for equal work has now become the general rule. In most cities, most educated and skilled women are employed as teachers, nurses, and assistants. Others areas where women find employment include banks, department stores, and government offices, where they are employed as administrative and clerical workers. They are also employed as domestic service providers.

In rural areas, women constitute a larger percentage of the workforce. The 1973 census revealed that only 14,000 rural women were economically active out of a total of 200,000 rural women older than age 10. In practical terms, many rural women were engaged in unpaid agricultural and domestic work that was not accounted for in the census figures. Estimates of the actual number of paid and unpaid female workers in rural areas in the mid-1970s were more than 86,000.

Under Qaddafi, other statutes regulated conditions, hours of work, and benefits for working mothers. These statutes sought to encourage women to, among other things, continue working, especially after marriage and childbirth. The types of incentives offered included cash bonuses and free childcare for their firstborn children. Women could retire as early as age 55. They were also entitled to gratuities and pensions.

Since the early 1960s, women in Libya have had the right to vote and hold office. However, the highest political position achieved has been one woman in the national cabinet in 1987. She was appointed Assistant Secretary for Information and Culture. Women are allowed to own property without recourse to their husbands, and they could also dispose of their property at will and without consulting their husbands.

Women's associations are prevalent throughout Libya, and in 1970, many feminist organizations came together to form the Women's General Union, which became the Jamahiriya Women's Federation in 1977. Women's movement in Libya are primarily concerned with issues of adult education and health.

The status of women in Libya has undergone considerable change since 1969. However, the impact of culture considerably impeded the government's efforts to improve the status of Libyan women.

Women and the Law

Libya inherited the majority of its contemporary legal system from the Ottomans. During Ottoman rule, a dual system of justice distinguished between secular matters and religious matters. For Muslims, cases relating to individual status and patrimony, such as marriage and inheritance, fell within the power of the Sharia courts. These courts were structured into two forms: the court of original jurisdiction and the court of appellate jurisdiction. An Islamic religious judge, called a *Qadi*, directed each of these courts. Secular matters, such as matters involving commercial, civil, and criminal laws, were not adjudicated in the Sharia courts but in a separate, secular court system. These secular courts were oriented toward the Western judicial tradition and emphasized an application of the Napoleonic Code. Muslims were subjected to the Sharia courts, while non-Muslims were subjected to the secular courts.

This dual court system was preserved by all imperial powers that governed Libya after the fall of the Ottomans. However, following Libya's independence, attempts were made to unify the two legal systems. In 1954, an attempted merger that relegated Islamic law under secular law met with intense resentment, and the move was shelved by 1958.

The 1969 revolution recognized certain fundamental tenets of the Western legal tradition, such as presumption of innocence, equality before the law, and right to inheritance. All of these were made subservient to Sharia law, and the revolution did little to develop Libya's legal system. In addition, its other constitutional declarations provided little direction for the postrevolution Libyan judiciary. It was not the courts that had ultimate legal authority; members of the Revolutionary Council had the power to cancel or decrease legal sentences by issuing decrees and to announce general amnesties. The Council also had the power to appoint judges to the courts, determine their tenures, and assess judges' performance. It also had the power to promulgate laws.

From the 1970s, the revolutionaries emphasized the supremacy of Islamic law, and they abolished the dual religious-secular court structure in favor of the secular court, which now has jurisdiction over religious matters. However, secular jurisprudence must conform with Sharia, which is regarded as the basis for religious and secular jurisprudence.

As of 1987, there were four levels to Libya's court system: summary courts, which are also known as partial courts; courts of first instance; appeals courts; and the Supreme Court. Unlike other countries, summary courts consistof one judge who heard misdemeanor cases in small towns. Primary courts are courts of first instance. As courts of first instance, they had, at minimum, a panel of three judges that rule by majority decision. The judges heard civil, criminal, and commercial cases, and they applied Sharia laws to personal and religious matters, They also heard appeals from summary courts.

There are three courts of appeal in the whole of Libya. These courts are in Tripoli, Benghazi, and Sabha. Like the primary courts, the courts of appeal have a three-judge panel and are ruled by majority to come to its decisions. They only hear appeals from the primary courts. In Libyan courts, original jurisdiction applies only to cases involving felonies and high crimes.

The Revolutionary Council insisted on appointing Sharia judges who have formerly served in the Sharia Court of Appeals to Libya's appeals courts. These judges, who specialize mainly in Sharia appellate cases, are appointed to serve in the regular courts of appeals where they continue to serve the state. The final court is the Supreme Court, which is located in Tripoli. The Supreme Court has five chambers: civil and commercial, criminal, administrative, constitutional, and Sharia. With a simple majority being the basis for establishing decisions, a five-member panel of judges sat in each of these chambers. The Supreme Court is the final appellate body, which hears cases emanating from the lower courts. In addition to the previously mentioned types of cases, the Supreme Court could also hears and interprets cases on constitutional matters. Despite the wide range of duties of the Supreme Court, it must be noted that it does not have the power to reverse the decisions of the lower courts, a power it had always exercised before the Qaddafi-led 1969 revolution.

Libya's legal system has passed through four broad stages: from Islamization to revolutionary legalism, to legality and human rights, and to a second period of Islamization. In the first stage, the regime moved to revive Islamic law and abrogate laws contrary to Islamic principles as part of a broader campaign to eliminate Western influence in Libya. In this period, Qaddafi emphasized his commitment to the Sharia law, although the legal system remained firmly anchored in the European civil law tradition. From April 15, 1973, emphasis shifted to a revolutionary transformation of Libyan society. Qaddafi set up a number of bodies that side-stepped the rule of law and all legal institutions, including Sharia, which might hinder the overhaul of society.

A combination of factors forced another legal reform. Internal political developments, including renewed tension between the regime and Islamist elements; foreign adventures, especially conflict in Chad; and tumbling oil revenues, reduced imports, and delayed development plans forced a retreat from revolutionary legalism to a third phase of legal policy that was characterized by an official respect for legality and human rights. At this time, Qaddafi turned into an advocate of legality, equality, freedom, human rights, and the rule of law, and he took note of various abuses that had taken place in Libya. Many state apparatuses, including the police, security service, and the Revolutionary Council, were roundly denounced as overzealous, reckless, and inimical to popular rule.

As if these reforms were not enough, in 1988, Qaddafi participated in the destruction of the central prison in Tripoli; supervised the destruction of police files collected by security forces; supervised the destruction of customs posts on the Tunisian border, declaring that all Libyans were now free to travel; and encouraged Libyan exiles to return home. In June 1988, he launched the Great Green Charter of Human Rights, which guaranteed some rights and freedoms that Libyans had not enjoyed before. The charter was progressive in some respects but fell short in guaranteeing freedom of conscience, freedom of worship, right to peaceful assembly, right to public trials, and prohibition of unlawful searches, among many others.

After 1990, Qaddafi's attention shifted to the economy, and he undertook steps to reduce state control of the economy, increase private sector participation, and curtail state spending. Qaddafi also proposed a form of popular participation that divided Libya into 1,500 self-governing communities. Each community would not only have its own executive and legislative arms but also its own budget. In practical terms, few of these laudable policies went beyond rhetoric. From 1993 to the 2011 revolution, a second stage of Islamization took place in Libya. In this fourth stage of legal development, which is characterized by an uneasy combination of Sharia law and *The Green Book*, the government cared little about the fundamental rights and freedom of Libyans.

Libyan laws guaranteed equality of the sexes and recognized no distinction between males and females. The revolutionary government left little doubt about its concern for the rights of women in Libya. At every turn in Libya's legal developments, the government enacted statutes that increased women's rights and checked freedoms culturally and religiously ascribed to men by custom and Islamic religion in matters of marriage and divorce. For instance, the law gave women increasing rights to seek divorce or separation by customary or legal means, most especially in cases of desertion or maltreatment by their husbands. One law forbid men from taking additional wives without first obtaining the consent of their first wives, and another law prohibits divorced men from marrying foreign women, even if such women are Arab women from another Arab country. Another associated law prohibits men in government employment from marrying non-Arab women. In addition, legislation prohibits forced marriages, especially of females to persons that are not of their choice. In cases involving minors, the laws allow minors to appeal and waive parental consents to courts, whose verdicts on such matters are nonnegotiable.

However, other laws undermined the regime's preference of Libyan women over non-Libyan women. For example, the children of Libyan men born abroad are eligible for Libyan citizenship even if their mothers are non-Libyans, whether or not these mothers are from Arab countries. The same does not apply to children born of Libyan mothers by non-Libyan men, even if these children desire Libyan citizenship.

Both sexes have the right to bring and argue cases in courts. Technically speaking, women and men are equal under the law, but in practice this is often not the case. Throughout the four stages of legal development in Libya, the state has intervened at different turns to protect women's status within a restrictive culture that had relegated them to the background. As earlier noted, to boost its legitimacy, the government has promoted more expansive and inclusive roles for women in Libyan society since 1969. In addition to the field of education, where efforts were in high gear to ensure increasing female enrollment in schools, other positive steps taken by the regime included legislating the same minimum age for marriage for females as for males. Libyan women were the first females in the Arab world to attend a military academy. A special facility was built exclusively for women on the outskirts of Tripoli. In addition, the regime established the General Union of Women's Association, a network of all organizations focused on employment opportunities for women.

A woman officer salutes with her sword during a training session at the Women's Military Academy in Tripoli. (AP Photo/Giulio Broglio)

In spite of the latitude given Libyan women under the law, society backs culture and traditional practices that place a higher premium on male children and constrain the freedoms afforded Libyan women by the law. For instance, because of Libya's conservative legal outlook, a woman cannot bring legal cases to court unless her husband or a male relative does so on her behalf.

The Veil

The use of veils, like the use of *hijabs* (or head scarf), is an important requirement in Islamic dress. Muslim women are expected to cover or conceal their faces and bodies from unwanted and unsolicited gazes, especially from males, as a means of preventing sexual attraction capable of leading males to sin. While the use of either the veil or hijab is not peculiar to Libya, it is one of the most contentious issues among Libyans because of debate about the extent of concealment and openness that Libyan Islamic clerics allow. In some parts of the Islamic world, most women need not wear a *burqa*, a piece of clothing that covers the body from head to toe, but simply a head scarf. In some other parts of the Islamic world, the situation is

A woman and her daughter wearing a mix of traditional and western clothing. (AP Photo/Manu Brabo)

different, as women are required to cover themselves completely, a situation that many Western scholars, commentators, and thinkers have decried. In any case, what amount of covering is required of women in Islam remains contested.

No secular law in Libya mandates the use of veils. Many Libyan women choose to wear veils because of a combination of Islamic religious requirements and social pressure. The trajectory of Libya's legal development noted previously shows that during the first and the fourth periods, the use of veils assumed greater prominence. However, a woman's employment status affects the use of the veil in Libya. For instance, in rural Libya where women are farmers, herders, and farmhands, the freedom required by such work discourages strict adherence to the use of either the hijab or veil. Women in urban centers also find hijabs and veils restrictive and not conducive to their work environments; the same is not necessarily true, however, of housewives living in cities. In any case, most women who wear veils in Libya wear veils that leave their faces exposed rather than completely covered.

The Libyan government actively discourages the wearing of *burqas* or *niqab*, which cover the entire body, as doing so is regarded as a sign of fundamentalism. Even among women who wear veils, they are used mainly when the women are outside their homes, that is, when they are out with friends in the city, heading to work, or outside of the family circle. In the house and with family members, Libyan women go unveiled. Urbanization, industrialization, and global trade have altered traditional veil use, even in the urban centers. It is not uncommon today to see a young Libyan woman wearing a veil with tight-fighting jeans and a tight-fitting shirt. More than anything else, the veil has become both a religious and fashion accessory in contemporary Libya. Women who chose to wear it for either cultural or religious reasons usually mix it with Western dress, thereby turning veils into just one part of a woman's wardrobe. There is not a uniform expectation to the practices surrounding the veil, especially in urban areas. As required in Islam, the purpose of veiling is to discourage sexual temptation; in contemporary Libya, veils have become one part of a woman's wardrobe.

Division of Labor

In both *The Green Book* and in traditional Islamic culture, the primary responsibility of women is to give birth and raise a family while men are expected to be responsible for their families by providing whatever ensures a comfortable living for them. Men are expected to earn a decent enough living to ensure that their families are comfortable. If a man is not able to do this, he is seen as a failure. This is one reason men are required to prove that they can provide for a second, third, or fourth wife before they are permitted to take on multiple wives. In the household, men are expected to do little; the manual labor and other household chores fall to the women. Women are expected to avoid the company of men other than family members or husbands. It is also frowned upon for women to have any job where they will come into contact with men who are not members of their families.

Even though women are supposed to focus on childbirth and childrearing, an economic recession and changes in perspective have made it so many women must work outside of their homes, particularly in the urban areas. While this does not excuse them from maintaining a clean and comfortable home, most working women in Libya work two jobs outside of the home. Many Libyan women have argued that these economic developments have impacted their roles as mothers and caregivers.

Family Honor

Traditionally, sociocultural and political lives in Libya centered on the individual's family. In fact, family loyalty overrides all other obligations. Attributed or ascribed status is far more important in sustaining social relationships than personal achievements. In addition, an individual's honor and dignity are subsets of his or her family's good reputation, most especially the honor of a family's women. In spite of legal provisions to the contrary, women play a secondary role in all aspects of Libyan life.

Although all family members are responsible for maintaining the family's honor by carefully living their lives in accordance with societal values so as not to bring shame upon the family, so much more is expected of women than men. For instance, females are expected to be virgins before marriage, and thereafter sexual fidelity is essential to maintaining their family's honor. However, no such demand is made of males.

One of the most visible ways a woman can bring shame upon a family is if she engages in premarital and/or extramarital affairs. The worst situation is if such affairs should lead to conception of a child out of wedlock. Virginity, especially for women, is prized; when a nonmarried female is discovered to have lost her virginity, it brings unbearable shame to the family. Cases abound of women cast out of the family for losing their virginity before marriage or having affairs (especially those leading to conception). The irony of such cases is that negative judgment is often rendered on unmarried pregnant women, regardless of how the woman got pregnant. In the case of a rape, for example, victims are often forced to marry their attackers as a way to safeguard the family's honor. Although Libyan laws forbid forced marriages, family and societal pressures often give raped women little or no choice.

Reproductive Rights

Birth control is legal in Libya; however, few Libyan women have the necessary education to take advantage of modern birth control methods. Therefore, the majority of Libyan women suffer from a lack of access to resources for reproductive health and birth control. The implications of are many. Libyan women tend to have more children than their counterparts in the West; they have little, if any, control over reproduction; and maternal mortality rates and associated problems are higher in Libya than might be expected. Abortion is illegal in Libya, and procuring one is punishable by imprisonment, even if it is used to remove an unwanted pregnancy that came about due to rape or incest. Women who can afford the cost often travel to other countries to access better medical care, including reproductive healthcare.

Note

1. Muammar al-Qaddafi, *The Green* Book, Tripoli, 1976, 111.

7

Social Customs and Lifestyle

ROLE OF THE INDIVIDUAL

IN LIBYA, EMPHASIS IS PLACED on the collective's interest in social relations. Individuality is often given up for the good of the largest group. Society views individuality as dangerous to the collective will, and it is dangerous to stand out as being different, especially in public. After Qaddafi seized power in 1969, his writings and decrees consistently affirmed that individuals had to concede their rights to the local ruling councils so that society could benefit from the collective knowledge and experience of everyone.

To ensure that individual rights are subsumed in favor of the group, the One September Revolution government provided almost all Libyans with housing, food allowances, and other necessities. In addition, the government nationalized many large companies and industries, including all banks throughout Libya. During the 1970s and 1980s, the government took a major stake in the banking system by abrogating all private savings accounts, making the population of Libya completely dependent on the government. As already noted, these measures ensure that the role and importance of the individual in Libyan society is subsumed within the needs of the larger society.

In Libya, the family, essentially the smallest unit of sociopolitical control in Libya, does a lot of activities together. For instance, dining together and taking daily tea together are family events that aim to build a collective rather

A boy throws stones to knock down seeds from a palm tree for his goat herd near Ghadames in western Libya. (AP Photo/John Moore)

than a personal or individual identity. Marriage in Libya, as in the whole of Africa, is more of a family affair than a personal one between couples. Individuals must live in ways that uphold family honor and pride.

EDUCATION

Education is an important part of Libyans' life. Libya's population includes 1.7 million students; more than 270,000 people are studying at the postsecondary level. Basic education is free for all Libyan citizens, and education is compulsory for all citizens up to the secondary school level. Because of these requirements, the literacy rate in Libya is among the highest in North Africa; well over 87 percent of the population is able to read and write.[1] Throughout much of Libya's history, only the elites of society were educated. The government provides a university education through a number of public universities. The largest publicly supported university in Libya is Al-Fateh University in Tripoli. After independence, in 1951, the government established the University of Libya in Benghazi. By the 1975 to 1976 academic year, the university's enrollment was estimated at about 13,418. By 2004, university enrollment throughout Libya increased to more than 200,000, and 70,000 additional students were enrolled in technical and vocational institutions. The rapid enrollment in higher education mirrored a corresponding increase in the number of higher education institutions in Libya. Students are able to attend public universities for free; however, private universities charge tuition.

By 1975, Libya had only 2 universities. By the 1980s, the number of universities in Libya had increased to 12 and included private universities as well as technical and vocational institutes. By 2000, the number of institutions for higher learning and vocational training stood at 84. Major Libyan universities include Al-Fateh University in Tripoli, Misrata University in Misrata, Garyounis University in Benghazi, and University of Omar Almukhtar in Al Bayda. Technology institutes that award degrees include the Higher Institute of Computer Technology and the Higher Institute of Electronics, both in Tripoli. The government finances most of the cost of Libyans' higher education. In 1998, the government allocated 38.2 percent of its budget to financing education.

Libya's investment in education can be traced to its colonial past. During both the Ottoman and Italian occupations; education was regulated by the colonial state, and education was made available only to the elites. The vast majority of the population was denied access to education. Therefore, after independence, the government guaranteed access to education for all Libyans, irrespective of location, political viewpoint, or socioeconomic status.

Among other things, Qaddafi's government viewed the government's school system as a way to educate the populace in traditional subjects and to instill revolutionary zeal. Teachers and students were regarded as vanguards of the revolution, and schools were used to indoctrinate students in state views and beliefs.

Until the revolution, education was reserved for males; female children were denied an education. Since the revolution, women have had equal access to education. In many parts of Libya, females attend schools longer than their male counterparts, and both sexes have almost equal representation at the universities. Qaddafi's government encouraged females to attend school and gain an education that would allow them enjoy equal opportunities in the job market and equality in status in Libyan society.

ECONOMY

The Libyan economy presents a curious spectacle that is unique within North Africa. Egypt, Algeria, Tunisia, and Morocco possess large populations, agricultural potential, and deep-rooted industrial bases. Libya's population is a comparatively paltry 6.355 million, according to a May 2011 report of the *World Population Prospects*. However, the nation is blessed with ample energy resources, especially its light, low-sulfur crude oil and natural gas. Libya's relatively small population and considerable income based on petroleum production makes it so the nation shares more characteristics with the oil-exporting nations of the Persian Gulf than it does with its North African neighbors.

The United Nations described Libya prior to independence as underdeveloped, backward, and the world's poorest nation. It feared that Libya would spend most of its early years of independence relying on generous international grants-in-aid until it was able to live within its meager means. This prediction proved false. Thanks to its abundant oil and gas deposits, Libya has evolved into a rapidly developing nation. Libya's accrued net gold and foreign exchange reserves are equivalent to more than US$4 billion; its estimated annual income from oil and gas revenues is between US$6 and US$8 billion.

Libya's postindependence economic progress has moved through four different developmental stages. The first stage began in 1951 with the nation's independence and included the 1957 discovery of crude oil in commercial quantities. This stage ended in 1961. The second stage began in 1961 and ended in 1969, when oil exports transformed Libya from a backwater country and placed it at the forefront of the world's major oil and gas economies. The beginning of the third stage began on September 1, 1969, with the military coup d'état that brought Qaddafi and his Free Officers' Movement into power. At this stage, Libya changed from a Western-oriented capitalist economy into a nationalist, anti-Western socialist state. Government interventions in the economy, which grew rapidly because of oil and gas revenues in the 1970s, were the major highlight of this stage. The fourth stage of Libya's economic development was characterized by a decline in the global oil trade that began in the early 1980s. During this stage, government revenues were dramatically reduced because of declining oil and gas accruals that necessitated a serious decline in the country's economic activities.

In general, the Libyan economy primarily depended on, and still primarily depends on, oil and gas revenues. Oil and gas revenues represent 95 percent of the nation's total export earnings and constitute 60 percent of the country's public sector wages. Low population and extensive revenues from oil trade gives Libya the highest per capita gross domestic product (GDP) of all African countries. In spite of these huge resources, most Libyans are extremely poor.

In the last decade, the government has carried out different types of economic reforms as part of a comprehensive effort to reintegrate the country into the political and economic fold of the West. These efforts became necessary after many years of global sanctions spearheaded by the United Nations, U.S. economic and military sanctions, and international isolation. These global sanctions relaxed in 2004 when Libya announced its intention to jettison its programs seeking to build weapons of mass destruction. Once international economic and military sanctions were removed, Libya attracted more direct, foreign investment, especially in its energy sector. Economic liberalism has since set the stage for a transition from a socialist state to a more market-based economy, and Libya has intensified efforts to reduce government subsidies and privatize businesses. Libya's nonoil sectors, especially manufacturing and construction, account for more than 20 percent of total GDP. The nonoil sectors have expanded outside of processing agricultural products to include the massive production of iron, aluminum, steel, and petrochemicals such as fertilizers. However, poor soil conditions and a harsh desert climate severely limit agricultural production; Libya continues to import more than 75 percent of its food supplies.[2]

Jobs

With a population of about 6.4 million people, Libya's official labor force is about 1.64 million, with a 30 percent unemployment rate. Libya's adopted socialist form of government required that the government employ all Libyans. Government agencies and intermediaries placed Libyans in jobs and provided job training. Increased urbanization and industrialization have drawn an influx of young men and women from the rural areas to the urban centers of Tripoli, Benghazi, and Tobruk. The emigration necessitated that the government provide employment for an ever-growing number of people because the economy could not keep up with the inflow of workers.

The government's inability to provide employment for youths pouring into the cities necessitated the creation of a social welfare system to take care of the basic needs of the population. In the early 2000s, Qaddafi's government began to adopt a free market system, seek to end economic sanctions, and encourage the develop of the private sector. They hoped that these changes would create new employment opportunities as increasing numbers of investors were attracted to Libya. Investors focused much of their attention on the energy sector. The tourism and service industries also are developing at a fast pace.

Throughout North Africa and the Middle East, a largely foreign workforce labors in the oil industry. The percentage of immigrants living in Libya is smaller than that of other Organization of the Petroleum Exporting Countries (OPEC) nations, but their presence is still a sensitive subject among many Libyans. The influx of immigrants and foreign laborers has raised ethnic and nationalist awareness in Libya, and unemployed Libyans have become resentful of immigrants.

A Libyan coppersmith hammers metal at Tripoli's old market. (AP Photo/Hussein Malla)

Unemployment is widespread in Libya; women are often underemployed and have a higher unemployment rate than men, although they are technically equal under the law. However, Libyan women have far more opportunities in Libya than in other Muslim countries, and many of them serve important roles in the economy. There are women doctors, pilots, artists, lawyers, business executives, and even soldiers.

PERSONAL RELATIONSHIPS

Traditional Libyan society is a strictly gendered society. Nonfamilial relationships with those of the opposite sex are culturally taboo; therefore, people cultivate friendships strictly along gender lines. Women and men cannot cultivate close relationships with nonblood relatives outside of marriage. Contemporary Libya is still conservative to a large extent but has witnessed enormous changes. Globalization and liberalization of the Libyan economy underlie some these developments.

Social life is traditionally centered on loyalty to one's individual family. More than any other responsibility, family relationships far outweigh other social relationships, and they regulate other social relationships. In most aspects of life and despite legal claims to the contrary, women still play secondary roles to men. Tradition prescribes that women remain in the home—sometimes in seclusion. However, the cities have become crucibles of social change and allowing women more and more freedom to work and form relationships in modern Libya.

Dating

Dating is frowned upon in traditional Libyan society given the conservative and Islamic nature of the country. In more traditional regions and groups, dating is forbidden, and marriages are usually arranged by parents. In most cases, couples have not met before their marriages are arranged. Where this is the case, couples generally spend time together in the company of their parents or other chaperones so that they know one another before the wedding ceremonies.

Marriage, as noted earlier, is more than a simple affair between a man and woman; it is a family, if not a community, affair. This is so because males and females, except members of the same family, rarely mix socially. Therefore, young men and women have less contact with each other, and relationships between the sexes seldom developed. Although marriages have always occurred outside of family circles, in the past most Libyans prefer marriages between children of brothers or close relatives to marriages with outsiders or people of different ethnic origins. Nomads, especially the Tuaregs, have a reputation for allowing much more freedom of choice in dating, courtship, and marriage.

However, increased urbanization and educational opportunities have altered this traditional practice because dating and courtship have developed as precursors to marriage in recent times. Young Libyans, especially educated city dwellers, have rejected the traditional practice of parents arranging marriages for their children. Young urban professionals now date before marriage and, rather than marry someone chosen by their families, they marry someone of their choice. The ongoing economic liberalization of the country has brought unmarried men and women into closer proximity to each other, especially in the workplace, leading to a continual transformation of traditional norms regarding coed relationships. Social contacts, especially in public, between unmarried men and women are still frowned upon, but increasingly more public contact between men and women has led to more avenues for social contact.

With respect to marriage, the government has enacted a number of statutes to improve the position of females in recent times. For example, to discourage child marriage, the government imposed a minimum age of 16 for females and 18 for males before any marriage can be contracted. In addition, marriage by proxy and forced marriage are forbidden by law. If parents forbid a young woman from marrying a man of her choice, the law allows the woman, even when she is a minor, to appeal to a court to prevent her parents from marrying her off to someone she does not want to be married to, and she may also seek the court's permission to marry a man of her choice.

Chastity

Until recently, Libyan society tenaciously held on to conservative attitudes and values about women, especially on issues of chastity and family honor. Women were regarded as the embodiment of a family's honor and worth. They must be modest, circumspect, and decorous. And their virtue must be above reproach. Virginity is regarded as not just a woman's property but also the property of her family. To maintain a family's honor, females must be virgins before marriage, and they must remain sexually loyal only to their husbands after marriage. Any errant behavior on the part of women is punished severely.

Although both the bride and groom are expected to be virgins on their wedding nights, Libyan society is more concerned about females' virginity than that of males. If it is discovered that a bride was not a virgin on her wedding night, she and her family are publicly scorned; the marriage cancelled; and the bride, her family, and most especially her mother are shunned. To preserve a family's honor, pride, and good name, most families prefer to marry off their daughters at the earliest age possible to ensure that they remain virgins before marriage. Paradoxically, if the male proves not to be a virgin, little is done to him or his family.

While Christians and other religious groups exist in Libya, but the majority of Libyans are Muslims. As enjoined by Muhammad, every Muslim must profess or testify that "There is no God but God Allah, and Muhammad is his Prophet." This is called the profession of faith, or the confession or testimony of faith (*shahadah*), which is a pillar of Islamic faith and a fundamental belief in Islam. A chaste, faithful, and pious Muslim repeats this simple profession of faith at intervals and at every religious occasion. In addition to the *shahadah*, there are four other tenets that Muslims must obey to be chaste before God. These are daily prayers or *salat*, almsgiving or *zakat*, fasting or *sawm* (most especially during the holy month of Ramadan), and going on holy pilgrimage to Mecca or *hajj*.

FUNERARY RIGHTS

As noted in the Chapter 6, Libyan Muslims are subject to Sharia law, which covers all aspects of life, including death. The Sharia law was developed from the Quran and by jurists using traditions of the Prophet Mohammad to construct a comprehensive code of human behavior.

Libyan burial rights, as in most of the Muslim world, follow traditional Islamic practices and require that a dead body be washed and wrapped in clean white linen before burial. In addition, dead bodies must be buried with the right side facing Mecca. Funerals and interment in Libya follow this simple Islamic tradition and are performed in strict accordance with the Quran. Interment is done as quickly as possible because Islam forbids embalming the body. No matter the circumstances surrounding death, autopsies are rarely performed. More often than not, interment is not so much a time for mourning but a time to worship; Muslims give thanks and prayers to Allah for the departed. According to Islamic law, only men are allowed to attend funeral and interment services. Women are allowed to express their grief only by wailing at the deceased's home.

The interment process begins with preparing the body. In Libya, like the rest of the Muslim world, the body is cleaned by family members. Women wash female corpses, and men wash male corpses. After it is washed, the body is wrapped in clean, unadorned, white cotton called *kafan*. There are strict rules about how this cloth is made. The *kafan* is wrapped from head to toe, making sure that the head is visibly marked. It is then taken to the place where the funeral prayers will be said. Here, an Imam leads others in prayers facing Mecca. After the prayers, the body is taken to the cemetery and buried without a coffin.

The deceased's grave is raised slightly, and tombstones or any other markers are frowned upon in Islam. The interment is designed not only to give closure to the family and friends but also to honor Allah. In Islam, cremation is forbidden, and the Quran maintains that breaking a deceased's bones is tantamount to breaking the bones of the living; hence, dead bodies are to be treated with the utmost respect. Three days of mourning follow the interment, and further prayers are said for the dead. The deceased's family receives visitors during these days. Elaborate dress, including the use of jewelry, is forbidden. Widows are expected to observe a much longer period of mourning, which lasts 4 months and 10 days. During this period, the widow is not to marry and is to refrain from contact with any male that she is not related to.

PARTICIPATION IN GOVERNMENT

Following the overthrow of King Idris and the Sanusi monarchy by Colonel Muammar Qaddafi and the Free Officers Movement on September 1, 1969, fundamental changes were introduced that transformed Libya. From the outset, Qaddafi articulated a unique ideology he termed the Third Universal Theory to serve as an alternative to capitalism and Marxism. This ideology was espoused in Qaddafi's three-volume *The Green Book* and calls for "direct democracy" in Libya. Qaddafi describes direct democracy as a government where the citizens govern through grassroots activism and without any intervention from the state, state institutions, or any other organizational hierarchies, such as the military, ethnic groups, religious leaders (especially the *ulama*), or the political intelligentsia. In his efforts to implement direct democracy, Qaddafi dismantled state institutions and social structures. In addition, in 1973, he launched a cultural revolution and, in 1975, instituted what he called the "people's power." In 1977, he proclaimed Libya a "state of the masses." To emphasize his policy of decentralization, Qaddafi finally dropped his own formal official title in 1979 and adopted the new title of Leader of the Revolution.

What is today Libya was historically divided into three provinces: Tripolitania is in the northwest, Barka or Cyrenaica in the east, and Fezzan in the southwest. These three separate provinces were fused and administered as one territory called the Territory of the Libyan Sahara following the Italian conquest, and four new provinces were created from the remaining provinces in the south. They included Tripoli, Misrata, Benghazi, and Al Bayda. After independence, Libya reverted to the previous three divisions and called them governorates or *muhafazat*. In 1963, the three governorates were divided into ten governorates. However, in February 1975, the ten governorates were replaced with nine "control bureaus." Each control bureau had ministries for education, housing, health, labor, social services, agricultural services, financial services, communications, and economy.

In 1983, the control bureaus were dismantled and, in their stead, Libya was divided into 46 districts called *baladiyat*. Over the next 2 decades, the districts were subdivided, expanded, and recombined. In 2007, the districts were further fragmented into congresses called the Basic People's Congresses, and they currently serve as townships or boroughs. These districts do afford Libyans an opportunity to participate in governance. However, the fact remains that only members of the Revolutionary Council are appointed to head the districts, and the appointees must be Qaddafi loyalists. Since the fall of Qaddafi, the Revolutionary Council has been abolished and Libyans are in the process of reordering their political structure.

Prior to Qaddafi's fall from power and eventual death, Libya's official state organs were the General People's Congress (GPC), which, as earlier noted, is composed primarily of members of the former Revolutionary Command Council (RCC). Qaddafi abolished the RCC in 1977. The GPC replaced the old Council of Ministers, which was also abolished in 1977. Like the old Council, the GPC performed the function of a cabinet. Qaddafi sat at the head of the GPC. The GPC performed executive and legislative functions and met only three times a year.

To facilitate people's representation and participation in government, three parallel committees with overlapping functions were established at the urban ward, rural village, and municipal levels. In addition to these three committees, the Arab Socialist Union (ASU), Basic Popular Congress (BPC), and revolutionary committees were organized along geographic lines. The ASU and BPC were the only authorized political mass organizations.

Although these bodies existed and were fully functioning, membership was determined not by popular will but by Qaddafi's will. The functions, responsibilities, and lines of authority of these bodies were so blurred that many have argued that Qaddafi designed them to ensure they were inefficient. Whatever the intent behind their creation, occasionally the ambiguous nature of the duties and responsibilities of these state organs resulted in intense antagonism and rivalry between the various organs of government. In practical terms, Libya was ruled exclusively by Qaddafi. Despite the fact that many Libyans participated in local government, the key decisions of the country were made by Qaddafi and his supporters.

Therefore, it was not surprising a great deal of resistance developed against Qaddafi's regime and leadership style. However, opposition to Qaddafi's rule was driven by different factors. In addition, opposition came in different forms and at different times. The first group to voice dissatisfaction with Qaddafi's rule was comprised of the wealthy, privileged, and traditional rulers whose power, function, and prestige under King Idris's government was respected and incorporated into governance. They resented Qaddafi's postrevolution government, and they were destroyed by it. The religious elites also resented Qaddafi's postrevolution government and felt he did not respect their powers, especially their roles as interpreters of the Quran. The ranks of the dissatisfied swelled with every step taken by the Qaddafi-led government and included some segments of the Libyan Armed Forces, university students, technocrats, intellectuals, and political leaders.

No discussion of popular resentment to Qaddafi's rule is complete without specific mention of the roles of the students and the army. The first group that supported the Qaddafi-led government and revolution were the students and the army. However, Qaddafi lost the students' support in 1976 when his government curtailed academic freedom by intervening in student unionism at the universities. In January 1976, students at the University of Benghazi protested government interference in their union elections following the government's cancellation of student elections. The student leaders were considered antigovernment. They were not members of ASU and were, therefore, considered unacceptable by the authorities. Government security forces quelled student demonstrations on the campus, a move that sparked further violence; the government adamantly denied reports that students were shot and killed or injured in the incident. Sympathizers organized more protests in Benghazi, Tobruk, and smaller towns and villages throughout Libya.

While manifestations of disaffection within the student populace were limited to protests within their schools, protests by the military remained the most potent and gravest threat to Qaddafi's regime. A major example of this threat is the Chad War. Faced with increasing numbers of casualties and setbacks, soldiers defected and deserted the army. At least six air force personnel, a lieutenant colonel, and many members of the armed forces fled to Egypt in March 1987. The defectors denounced Qaddafi's rule and requested asylum in Egypt. Qaddafi's attempt to replace the regular armed forces with a people's army and the interference of the various committees in national security matters were other sources of disaffection within the armed forces.

Under Qaddafi's reign, various laws and decrees were created to limit political activities like forming political parties. The most important legal statutes included the Decision on the Protection of the Revolution of December 1969, the Penal Code, and Law No. 71 of 1972. Taken together, these laws made political activities in Libya strictly illegal and forced any opposition to flee the country or go underground. A breach of any of these laws, especially where such activity was regarded as a direct threat against the state, carried a death penalty. Academics and others in Libya were allowed to join only nonpolitical international societies or associations; they had to procure the express written permission of the state to join, and membership without prior approval was punishable by imprisonment. A similar fate awaited anyone who insulted the Constitution, the Libyan flag, or popular authorities.

The following actions were considered crimes against the government and punishable by death: violently or forcefully attempting to change the government, attempting to subvert the Constitution, advocating any theory or principle aimed at changing the government or the constitution of Libya, and forming any group without official permission from the government. When Qaddafi announced the Cultural Revolution in April 1973, he announced that promoting conservatism, atheism, capitalism, Islamic fundamentalism (especially the Muslim Brotherhood), or communism were punishable only by death.

To stifle opposition, Qaddafi made it clear that his government would brook no opposition. Opposition, he declared, was harmful to Libya's national unity. Speaking in October 1969, Qaddafi, stated that Libya needed "national unity free of party activities and division" and that "he who engages in party activities commits treason."[3]

Despite legal strictures and physical attempts to destroy opposition to his government, resistance to Qaddafi remained and later killed him. In December 1969, a plot involving two cabinet ministers who wanted to eliminate Qaddafi was uncovered. A second plot, involving King Idris's distant cousin, was also uncovered in July 1970. In addition, traditional leaders of various ethnic groups mounted protests against Qaddafi. These leaders had been displaced by the Qaddafi-led government or were about to be displaced by the so-called government administrators, modernizing technocrats, popular congresses, and the numerous people's committees set up by Qaddafi.

While it may appear that Qaddafi favored the modernizing technocrats to the former traditional rulers, numerous technocrats and many others from the urban population also opposed Qaddafi. They especially opposed his emphasis on religion, which he also grossly undermined. The *ulamas*, the traditional Islamic religious leaders, also opposed Qaddafi because of his opposition to their intermediary and interpretive functions.

Amidst political skepticism about his government, Qaddafi was able to maintain his hold on government through petroleum wealth. Basic social services were provided by the government, and a large portion of the Libyan population remained ambivalent toward Qaddafi's government.

IMPACT OF THE WEST ON LIBYAN CULTURE

In all aspects of life, from culinary and sartorial traditions to architecture and political development, the developments in contemporary Libya are due, in part, to the impact and influences of Western, Arab and Islamic cultures. Complementing these external influences is the resilience of the Libyan people, which serves as the pedestal upon which these changes and developments revolve. These developments began long before the Italian occupation.

The impact of the Romans and Greeks has been mitigated over the centuries, while the impact of the Italians in the early twentieth century remains today mostly in food and architectural designs. The impact of Western education, economic liberalization, industrialization, and globalization has made an indelible impact on Libya. Information and technology changes, industrialization and global trade, public healthcare, and a legal system that recognizes human rights have stimulated growth in the population of Libya as well as in education and the standard of living.

In addition to the factors mentioned in the preceding paragraph, educational opportunities have widened. School enrollment continues to increase, and more women are in the workplace than were there at independence. After the imposition of sanctions on Libya in the 1980s, Qaddafi banned English from being taught in schools as well as English language books and movies. However, since 2006, after the ban was lifted, English has been taught everywhere in Libya, which has allowed Libyan youth to begin to compete favorably with others in the world. Since 2005, Western media has began broadcasting, although in limited runs, everywhere in Libya. The cities are brimming with educated youth, most of whom wear Western style clothing.

In contemporary Libya, two sartorial traditions predominate. On the one hand, cultural hybridity involves the mixture of Western cloths with traditional Libyan clothes. It is common to see Libyan girls with brightly colored dresses, and boys wearing jeans and tee-shirts. Wearing Western clothes does not prevent young men from wearing skullcaps and females from continuing to cover their hair. These young people do so not so much because of religious reasons but more as a function of fashion. Libyans (mostly adults, and especially women) also wear purely Islamic dress.

Economic liberalization and global trade have stimulated labor migration and the importation of Western industrialists into Libya. A majority of these expatriates work in the energy sector. The benefit of these labor migrants and expatriates is not simply that they bring technical skills previously lacking in Libya but also that they open Libya to cultures other than theirs and make more knowledge of Libya available to other parts of the world.

LIBYAN HOLIDAYS

In addition to secular holidays that were tied to the 1969 revolution, Libyans mainly commemorate religious holidays. Although a number of non-Muslims live in Libya, only Islamic holidays are officially observed. The major Muslim holidays are *Eid el-Fitr*, which marks the conclusion of Ramadan, a month of fasting, and *Eid el-Adha*, which commemorates the willingness of Abraham to obey Allah's command that he sacrifice his only son to Allah. Other holidays are the Prophet Muhammad's birthday, Islamic New

Libyans enjoying a game of beach soccer. (AP Photo/Sergey Ponomarev)

Year, and the Tenth of Muharram, which is a day commemorating when Moses led the Israelites out of Egyptian slavery.

As noted earlier, only secular holidays related to the 1969 revolution were respected and observed in Libya under Qaddafi. It will be interesting to see how the holiday schedule in Libya will change as the nation puts Qaddafi behind it. A few of those holidays include Independence Day (December 24); Revolution Day (September 1); Evacuation Day (June 11), which marks the commemoration of the United States withdrawing from Wheelus Air Force Base; Army Day (August 9); and Proclamation Day (November 21).

As do other nations of the world, Libya places great importance on its holidays. Unlike religious holidays that are either tied to specific developments in Islamic history or are made compulsory by Prophet Mohammad, both religious and secular holidays are celebrated by most people in Libya. Religious minorities do not celebrate Muslim holidays; rather, they celebrate their own holidays (e.g., Christians celebrate Christmas) within their own communities. However, the most important holidays in the country are those associated with Islam. Since almost everyone in Libya is Muslim, Islamic holidays are officially celebrated by both individuals and the government.

NOTES

1. UN Statistics Division, "Social Indicators," accessed online on August 3, 2011, available at http://unstats.un.org/unsd/demographic/products/socind/literacy.html

2. Central Intelligence Agency, "World Factbook, Libya," available online at www.cia.gov/library/publications/the-world-factbook/geos/ly.html

3. Quoted in Helen Chapin Metz, "Opposition to Qadhafi," *Libya: A Country Study* (Washington: G.P.O. for the Library of Congress, 1987), accessed online on August 3, 2011, available at http://countrystudies.us/libya/76.htm

8

Music and Dance

MUSIC

As NOTED IN CHAPTER 5, Libya was, for many years, conquered, occupied, and administered by outsiders who left behind multidimensional legacies. From the Phoenicians to the Greeks, the Romans to the Spaniards, the Ottomans to the Italians, Libya have different and, oftentimes, conflicting heritages. While the Greeks and Romans were pagans and animists, the Ottomans were Muslims, and the Spaniards and Italians were Christians. After a few years under the United Nations' watch, Libya became an independent nation with barely any hope of survival until the discovery of crude oil. The imprints left by these outsiders are some of the defining features of contemporary Libyan culture.

Many are quick to describe Libya's dance and musical heritages as primarily Arabic. This is an oversimplification. On the surface, it may appear as if little or nothing is known or could be known about traditional Libyan culture in music and dance before the Phoenicians Actually, Libya's musical heritage is a mixture of Arabic, Berber, and Spanish musical cultures. Conservatively, it could be argued that traditional Berber music has mutated over the years or has been merged into imported cultures. However, traditional Libyans did possess an indigenous music, and traces of it still exist. While Neolithic artifacts and other archaeological finds have pointed to different cultural elements in Libyan music and dance, details such as what materials the items were made of, the kinds of music they produced, and what sort of dances accompanied the music are probably lost forever.

Arabs are the most populous ethnic group in Libya; hence, Libyan music and dance appear to be largely Arabic in nature. However, Berber and Andalusian musical cultures also exist. Also, traces of Tuareg music are to be found in Libya. The Tuaregs in southern Libya, the Saharan part of Libya, have their own distinguishing traditional music, which is characterized by a great assortment of drums and a one-stringed, violin-like instrument called the *anzad*. Among the Tuaregs, women are predominantly the musicians.

Berber music, predominantly a village and urban folk music, varies across North Africa. Berber music is stylistically diverse, with the songs being predominantly African rhythms and a stock of oral literature. Berber musical instruments range from the *oboe* to bagpipes, which are used in making pentatonic music, which has five notes per octave scale. Berber musicians fall into two groups. One group is small bands of traveling musicians who move from one village to another entertaining people at ceremonies such as christening, funerals, weddings, and other social events with their songs, tales, and poetry. The second group consists of teams, ranging from 20 to 150 professional musicians.

In both groups, Berber music is usually accompanied by a rhythm section that consists of a tambourine, frame drum (*bendir*), and a melody section (which consists of a bagpipe [*ghaita*] and a flute [*ajouag*]). This music still exists within traditional Libyan communities. Unlike the West African call-and-response music style, Tuareg and Libyan Berber music uses rhythms and vocal styles similar to the music of other Berbers and Arabs.

Besides Tuareg and Berber music, Andalusian classical music also exists in Libya. This type of Moorish music can be found throughout almost all of North Africa and southern Spain. Although the music is now closely linked with Algeria and southern Spain, similar musical traditions abound in Morocco, Tunisia, and Libya. However, Andalusian classical music in Libya is heavily influenced by both Ottoman and Berber music, most notably the *Chawi* music from the Constantine region. In addition, *huda*, reputed to be a traditional camel driver's song, is spread daily by traveling Bedouin poet-singers and has thus become popular across Libya. *Huda* is called a camel driver's song because its rhythm appears to mimic the gait of a walking camel

As in other parts of the world, Libyan music is both secular and religious, and both forms are equally important in Libyan culture. While secular music is mostly consumed by youths, especially educated urban dwellers, religious and traditional music is enjoyed by the older generations. Today, it is the Egyptians who are having the most profound effect on Libya's musical culture. Egyptian musicians are the most popular musicians in Libya, as they are throughout North Africa and southwest Asia. Libya's musical world is dominated by outsiders. Local Libyan artists have spurned both traditional and contemporary Arab genres. While pop and rap are strictly enjoyed by the youth, older generations of Libyans tend to listen to traditional and deeply religious Arab music.

Libyan music also varies from region to region, and each city and province has its own musical style and heritage. The Arab culture of the Middle East has strongly influenced eastern Libya's musical heritage. Southern Libya has a large sub-Saharan African influence, and western Libya bends toward Tunis and western North Africa. In addition to regional differences, influences, and peculiarities, rural-urban migration has also led to the evolution of different genres.

Traditional Libyan music, unlike Western music, relies on a homophonic sound rather than a polyphonic sound. Western music is based on harmony, with artists singing different parts within a song. In Libyan traditional music, all participants sing the same tone and, rather than harmonize, they focus on the melody and rhythm of the song. The result is a melody with different sounds based on unity rather than dueling voices or parts. In addition, Libyan music has a much larger tonal scale than Western music. The tonal scale, called *maqam*, has 24 different notes, while the chromatic scale used in Western music has only 12.

Libyan music also shares musical instruments, beats, and messages with outsiders who have occupied and ruled Libya. Many Libyans, especially Arabs, believe that Ottoman musical instruments were incorporated into Libyan musical traditions. Examples of these instruments include the *zokra*, which is a kind of bagpipe; the bamboo flute; the tambourine; a fretless lute called *oud*; and the *darbuka*, a goblet drum that is usually held sideways and played with the fingers. The *imzad* or *amzad* is used by the Tuaregs across North Africa; it is a single-stringed, bowed instrument used primarily by women. In addition, intricate clapping is found in almost all Libyan folk music.

Other musical instruments include the traditional violin, which locals call the *rebec*; its name is believed to have been derived from the word "rebab," whose original source is believed to be Arabic. The guitar is also popular and is locally called *qitara*. A small drum similar to Europe's kettledrum is called a *naker*, whose name was also derived from an original Arabic drum called the *naqareh*. The *adufe* is a Moorish, square-shaped tambourine predominantly used in Portugal, and it is called *al-duff* in Libya. Another important musical instrument commonly used in Libya is the *alboka*, which is a type of native clarinet that has two horns: the *anafil*, from the word "*al-nafir*," and the *exabeba*, which is derived from the word "*al-shabbaba*."

They are both different types of flutes. Other flutes often used in Libya include the *balaban* and the very popular *sonajas de azófar*, a kind of wind instrument with a characteristic cone-like shape. The *xelami* is a notable flute, or, more appropriately, a musical pipe that derived its name from the *sulami* or *fistula*. The *atabal* is a type of bass drum. Originally called *al-tabl*, it remains a popular musical instrument that can be found in most of urban and rural Libya. The *shawm*, like the *dulzaina*, is also a musical instrument made from reed. The *gaita*, originally from Spain and Portugal, is a king of bagpipes. It probably made its way into Libya via Spanish conquest and domination. The same could be said of *geige,* which is a German violin.

Whether locally made or imported, almost all instruments in Libya require specialized training before they can be used. The *oud*, which is of Arabic origin, is a pear-shaped stringed instrument similar to the lute. It is distinguished from other stringed instruments by its lack of a fretted neck, its 11 strings, and a peg box that is bent back at a 45- to 90-degree angle from the neck of the instrument. The *oud*'s body has a bowl-like shape in the back, which resembles a half watermelon that is turned inside out—unlike the back of a normal guitar, which is usually flat. The *oud*'s bowl design allows it to resonate and achieve a unique tonal quality. The shape, peculiar as it may appear, is structurally strong and stable despite its thinness. Although the *oud* is made of dense hardwood, it is a light instrument. This instrument, which is played with a pick, is perhaps the most popular musical instrument in the Arab and Muslim musical world.

Another popular instrument is the *tabla*, which is a set of two drums that can be made from wood, metal, or clay and covered with a leather band. The *tabla* can be played with either the hand or a small hammer. This table or goblet drum is found everywhere in North Africa and is not peculiar to Libya. Another type of goblet drum is the *darbuka*, which like the *tabla* is also played with the hand and produces a sharp beat. Musicians roll their fingertips off the drum to produce either quick or slow rhythms, depending on the song. Like the *tabla*, the *darbuka* is also made of clay, metal, or wood.

Unlike either the *tabla* or the *darbuka*, the *zokra* is a reed instrument, a predecessor to the oboe. The *zokra* is a long cylindrical instrument with a progressively widening opening toward the bottom. It has a double reed but no keys. It is played by blowing into the reed, and it produces a high-pitched note. It is the only instrument in the region to have a double reed. It is unclear if the *zokra* is an adaptation of the oboe.

In most of Libya's urban centers, the popularity of Arab pop music is increasing. As noted previously, pop and rap music consumed in Libya is produced mostly in Egypt, but some Libyan musicians have helped spur a

growth in homegrown pop and rap music. Libyan pop has become so successful that Ayman al-Aathar won the Mid-East Pop Award in 2004 in an
American Idol–type show called *Superstar* that was produced in Lebanon.

Libyan pop music is a blend of Western and Arab pop music that took
shape in the 1970s. It combines the use of electric guitars, keyboards, and
other American musical instruments with local Arab musical instruments to
create a unique but familiar Libyan sound. Arab pop songs generally focus
on issues of love, loss, and hardship, much like American pop music.

Over the last decade, rap and hip-hop music has emerged all over Libya. It
is predominantly sung and listened to by youths in the cities and, increasingly, in rural areas too. This rise in rap has caused a phenomenal shift in traditional Libyan music; many think rap has a negative influence on Libyan
youth. Until the 2011 political uprisings, Libyan rap was vulgar and concentrated on themes of sex and violence. With the uprising to unseat Qaddafi,
Libyan rap detoured into a form of protest music that focused on traditional
Islamic messages and encouraged people to live a clean and holy life. Prior to
the uprising, the nature of Qadaffi's regime prevented rap artists from using
this genre as an outlet for anger and frustration as it is used in the West.
One of the pioneers of Libyan pop is Ahmed Fakroun. Fakroun is trained
in both Arabic and Western styles of music, and he was one of the first in
the Arab world to create what is called Arabic World Music, which is a blend
of Western and Arab music.

Music of the Arab Spring

With the uprising to unseat Qadaffi's regime that began in Spring 2011, a
new form of music was developed within Libya and by Libyan exiles around
the world. This music directly supports the Libyan people's desire for democracy within Libya. The birthplace of the Music of the Arab Spring, as it is
famously called, was Benghazi, the city where the political uprising began.
It focuses on themes of redemption, perseverance, and justice for Libya.
Many of the songs were sung in both Arabic and English, and their target
audience was both those inside of Libya and also the outside world. The
music attempted to explain what was going on within the country.

One of the most important English language songs of the revolution was
"We Will Never Surrender," a rock ballad by Jasmine Ikanovic and Hussein
Kablan. This song was written shortly after the liberation of Benghazi and
is a testament to the fortitude and sacrifice of those who gave their lives in
opposition to Qadaffi's regime. It was hoped that the song would inspire
the Libyan people, at home and abroad, to continue their resistance and that
it would inspire the world community to help Libyans who were striving for a
world without Qadaffi.

Although "We Will Never Surrender" was a popular ballad, the music of the modern revolution in Libya is rap. Rap encapsulates the general anger and resistance toward authority, and it has helped to inspire those fighting. Dozens of rap songs from artists such as Wael el Warfali, Mohmmed el Banone, Imad Abbar, and Music Masters are played daily on free Libyan radio stations. These artists called for the overthrow of Qadaffi's regime and encouraged those fighting to destroy Qadaffi, who they described as the worst traitor in Libyan history. The youth of Libya have embraced this new form of music that has only recently entered the Arab world.

DANCE

Dancing in Libya usually coincides with religious celebrations. Due to the Islamic and conservative outlook of the country, men and women do not dance with each other in Libya. Males can dance with only fellow males, and females with fellow females if in the same hall and at the same time. It is customary in Libya for women to dance in the center of the hall and for men to dance in a ring around them. Dance often includes props such as swords. One of the most famous dances in Libya is *El Hagalla*, which women traditionally perform at weddings. *El Hagalla* is similar to the Western belly dance; the Libyan dance focuses more on the movement of hips, legs, and arms than the belly.

The Tuaregs in southern Libya dance to celebrate all manner of occasion and, like their Arab neighbors to the north, they dance strictly along gender lines. The Tuaregs not only bring in props but also camels in their famous camel dance, which celebrates the history and culture of the nomadic groups. A unique dance called *Guedra* is a form of Berber ritual dance, and it is common among the Touregs. *Guedra* is a ritualistic dance and is exclusive to women; it is usually done while kneeling. *Guedra* is not just a dance but also a ritual that involves everybody. It aims at creating energy, peace, and spiritual love.

Glossary

African Union (AU) A continental body of African states and successor of the Organization of African Unity (OAU).

Amir Literally, a commander or a chieftain of an independent Muslim community.

Aouzou Strip A territory in northern Chad, paralleling Libya's southern border and believed to be rich in valuable minerals, including uranium. It was first occupied by Libya in 1973 and later annexed in 1976.

Arab Socialist Union (ASU) A mass organization that was created in 1971 to provide a framework for popular participation and representation within the political system. From 1975, it was reorganized to include local-level Basic Popular Congresses (BPCs) and the lower-level Municipal Popular Congresses (MPCs). Prior to its disbandment in January 1976, both congresses sent delegates to the national General People's Congress (GPC).

Baath Another name for the Arab Socialist Resurrection Party, a pan-Arab party established in Damascus by Michel Aflaq and Salah ad Din al Bitar in the 1940s.

Baathist A member of the Baath party.

Baladiyat An administrative zone in Libya

Bani rabic for a tribe, a people, or a nation.

Baraka Quality of blessedness; grace, especially found in *marabouts* and other divinely favored persons, or charisma, which endows individuals with special capacity to rule.

Burqa A kind of dress, usually a full-length covering, used by Arabic and Islamic women.

Caliph   Literally a successor to the Prophet Muhammad. In contemporary usage, it refers to a spiritual and temporal leader of the Islamic community.

Cultural Revolution   One of the basic components of the Popular Revolution proclaimed on April 15, 1973. Cultural revolution was one of the major government policies under the deposed leader, colonel Qadaffi, which aimed at effacing foreign cultural influence and reviving Libya's Arab and Islamic heritage.

Cyrenaica   Occupying the eastern half of the country, Cyrenaica is one of the largest historic regions in Libya. It derives its name from the ancient Greek city-state, Cyrene, which is called Barqu in Arabic.

Dey   Literally maternal uncle, but used to refer to a junior officer that is commanding a company of janissaries. However, from 1611, it has been used to describe the head of government in Tripolitania.

Dhabiha   The Islamic ritualistic way of killing or slaughtering animals to make them qualified as *halal*.

Divan   A council of senior military officers during the Ottoman period.

Fezzan   One of Libya's three historic regions, located in the southwestern part of the country.

Free Officers Movement   A secret organization of junior Libyan army officers and enlisted men who carried out the September 1, 1969, coup against King Idris. Colonel Qadaffi was a member of this organization.

FROLINAT   Front de Liberation Nationale du Tchad (Front for the National Liberation of Chad); a Muslim insurgent movement supported by Libya.

General People's Committee   A name given to the cabinet (formerly the Council of Ministers) in March 1977.

General People's Congress   A body combining executive and legislative functions of government under the deposed leader, Colonel Qadaffi. It became the formal supreme organ of government in March 1977.

The Green Book   The first volume was published in 1976 and the second in 1978; it was Colonel Qadaffi's ideological testament, which contains his political, economic, and social thought, as well as revolutionary precepts and a definition of Arab socialism.

Habus   Sometimes written as *habous* or *hubus*; describes any Islamic religious endowment or trust (usually real estate), usually used to support mosques, schools, and other charitable works.

Hadith   Literally a speech or prophetic tradition; describes Islamic writings containing the sayings and teachings of Prophet Muhammad as recalled by his followers.

Hajj   One of the Five Pillars of Islam, which states that all Muslims, if they are able, must travel to Mecca at some point in their lives.

Halal   Lawful or religiously allowed; generally used in reference to food. Its opposite is *haram*.

Haram Forbidden or religiously disallowed; generally used in reference to food. Its opposite is *halal.*

Ibn Literally son of; used before or as part of a proper name to indicate patrilineal descent.

Ikhwan Professed members of a religious order resident in a *zawiya;*.usually translated as brothers.

Imam Generally, an Islamic leader who is a recognized authority on Islamic theology and law; also the prayer leader of a mosque. The term is used to designate the leader of the Islamic community in a particular locality.

Jamahiriya An Arabic word that has no official translation but unofficially means state of the masses, people's authority, or people's power. On March 2, 1977, Qadaffi officially declared Libya as the Socialist People's Libyan Arab Jamahiriya.

Janissaries Originally *yeniceri*, a Turkish word that means a new soldier; later used to describe members of an elite Ottoman military corps that were, first, recruited from among Turkish peasants. The soldiers were committed to a life of service during Ottoman rule.

Jihad In Islamic doctrine, a permanent struggle to establish the law of Allah on earth, often interpreted to mean holy war.

Jinns Supernatural creatures in Islamic folklore.

Jizya A tax allowed by Islamic law, as a penalty on non-Muslims living within an Islamic country. Non-Muslims are allowed to live and practice their faith as long as they pay this mandatory tax.

Khouloughli Literally sons of servants or sons of slaves; a distinct caste of mixed Turkish and Arab parentage, commonly found in Tripolitania.

Libyan Dinar (LD) A unit of currency introduced on September 1, 1971, by the Qadaffi-led government. It replaced the Libyan pound, which was in use before independence. The Libyan dinar is divided into 1,000 dirhams.

Maghrib Literally the time or place of the sunset or the west; describes areas along the western Islamic world (northwest Africa), as different from the *Mashriq,* and eastern Islamic world (the Middle East). Arabs describe the areas as the Island of the West (*jazirat al maghrib*), or the land between the sea of sand (Sahara) and the Mediterranean Sea. It traditionally includes Algeria, Morocco, Tunisia, and Tripolitania.

Mahdi Literally the enlightened, a divinely guided one or a religious leader who is recognized in Islamic tradition as a messiah ordained by Allah to unify Islam and institute a reign of virtue in anticipation of the last day.

Marabout A holy man and a teacher who is believed to be touched by divine grace (*baraka*) and therefore venerated. In addition to teaching and proselytizing, he also arbitrates tribal disputes.

Mauretania Original name for the ancient Berber kingdom in the northwest African and Roman provinces that succeeded it; different from the modern Islamic Republic of Mauritania.

Medina   Arabic, literally a town or city; used in North Africa to describe the old center of a city.

Minbar   A pulpit used in a mosque.

Moufflan   A wild and rare sheep, commonly found in Libya.

Muhafazaat (singular, muhafazat)   Although abolished in 1975, governorates or an administrative zone into which Libya's three traditional regions were divided in 1963.

Nasserism   The teachings of former Egyptian leader Abdul Nasser, particularly his belief in pan-Arabism.

Niqab   A garment worn by Muslim women that almost completely covers their face.

Organization of Arab Petroleum Exporting Countries (OAPEC)   A body that coordinates petroleum policies of major oil-producing Arab states. Membership includes Algeria, Bahrain, Egypt, Iraq, Kuwait, Libya, Qatar, Saudi Arabia, Syria, and the United Arab Emirates.

Organization of Petroleum Exporting Countries (OPEC)   An organization that coordinates petroleum policies of 13 major oil-producing countries. Members include Algeria, Ecuador, Gabon, Indonesia, Iran, Iraq, Kuwait, Libya, Nigeria, Qatar, Saudi Arabia, the United Arab Emirates, and Venezuela.

Pasha   In Tripolitania, the title of the regent representing the sultan; also describes an Ottoman provincial governor or military commander.

Qadi   A judge of a Sharia court.

Quran   The holy book of Islam.

Revolutionary Command Council (RCC)   The supreme organ of the revolutionary regime from September 1969 to 1977.

Revolutionary Committees   Unofficial spy organizations whose members tended to be devoted to Qadaffi and his teachings. They were organized in November 1977 to supervise the Basic People's Congresses and to fight bureaucracy, but over the years, they grew in importance so that their members selected delegates to the General People's Congress.

Salat   One of the Five Pillars of Islam that states that all Muslims must pray five times a day.

Shahadah   Literally testimony of the profession of the Islamic faith: "There is no god but God (Allah), and Muhammad is His Prophet."

Sharia   Islamic law, both civil and criminal, based on the Quran and the *hadith*. Other sources of this law include consensus of Islamic belief, consensus of the authorities on a legal question, and analogy or elaboration of the intent of law.

Sheikh   A tribal leader; also written as *sheik* or *shaykh*.

Shia Literally a party, for instance Shiat Ali (Party of Ali). This is the smaller of the two great divisions of Islam. Adherents, who are referred to as Shias, believed that the Quran is not a closed body of revelation but is open to further elaboration by inspired imams.

Shurfa The descendants of the Prophet Muhammad through his daughter, Fatima. In its broadest sense, *Shurfa* describes persons or groups with or having noble status.

Sultan Considered the ultimate secular title for a Muslim ruler, the title originally referred to the Almoravid, Hafsid, and Ottoman overlords of Libya.

Sunna A body of customs and practices based on the Prophet Muhammad's words and deeds as found in the Quran and the *hadith*, which serve as guides to proper behavior for Muslims.

Sunni This is the larger of the two great divisions of Islam. The Sunni consider themselves the orthodox adherents of the *sunna*.

Suq A traditional North African bazaar-like open-air market.

Third International Theory The major tenet of Qadaffi's revolutionary ideology, which claims to offer the Third World alternative political, economic, and social ideologies to from the Cold War dynamic of East vs West. Alternative names include the Third Universal Theory and the Third Theory.

Tripolitania Derived from the name Tripolis, which means the Three Cities. It is situated in the northwestern part of the country and is the most populous of Libya's three historic regions.

Ulama (singular, alim) Collective term for Muslim religious scholars who are learned in the Quran and are therefore responsible for interpreting and elaborating on Sharia.

Vilayet An administrative division of the Ottoman Empire, usually governed by a governor general called *wali*.

Wali A governor general of a *vilayet* during the Ottoman rule.

Zakat One of the Five Pillars of Islam, which requires all Muslims to give alms to the poor.

Zawiya (plural, zawaayaa) A lodge containing mosque, school, and quarters for *Ikhwan*, a religious order discussed previously.

Bibliography

BOOKS

Abd al-Mawlá, Maḥmūd. *Jihâd et colonialisme: La Tunisie et la Tripolitaine (1914–1918)*. Tunis: Ed. Tiers-Monde, 1987.

Abrahams, Fred. *Words to deeds: The urgent need for human rights reform*. New York: Human Rights Watch, 2006.

Aḥmar, al-Mawlidī. *Social roots of the modern Libyan state*. (Edition al-Ṭabah 1). Beirut: Markaz Dirāsāt al-Waḥdah al-Arabīyah, 2009.

Ahmida, Ali Abdullatif. *The making of modern Libya: State formation, colonization, and resistance, 1830–1932*. Albany: State University of New York Press, 1994.

Ahmida, Ali Abdullatif. *Forgotten voices: Power and agency in colonial and postcolonial Libya*. New York: Routledge, 2005.

Alawar, Mohamed A. *A Concise bibliography of northern Chad and Fezzan in southern Libya*. Outwell, Cambridgeshire, England: Arab Crescent Press, 1983.

Albergoni, G. et al. *La Libye nouvelle: Rupture et continuité*. Paris: C.N.R.S., 1975.

Albright, David E. *Peddling peril: How the secret nuclear trade arms America's enemies*. New York: Free Press, 2010.

Allan, J. A. *Libya since independence: Economic and social development*. New York: St. Martin's Press, 1982.

Al-Qasem, Anis. *Principles of petroleum legislation: The case of a developing country*. London: Graham and Trotman, 1985.

Amal, Obeidi. *Political culture in Libya*. Richmond, Surrey: Curzon, 2001.

Anderson, G. Norman. *Sudan in crisis: The failure of democracy*. Gainesville: University Press of Florida, 1999.

Anderson, Lisa. *The state and social transformation in Tunisia and Libya, 1830–1980.* Princeton, NJ: Princeton University Press, 1986.

Antoun, Richard T. *Law and Islam in the Middle East.* Santa Barbara, CA: ABC-CLIO, 1990.

Arnold, Guy. *The maverick state: Gaddafi and the New World Order.* New York: Cassell, 1996.

Askew, William Clarence. *Europe and Italy's acquisition of Libya, 1911–1912.* Durham, NC, Duke University Press, 1942.

Attir, Mustafa O. *Trends of modernization in an Arab society: An exploratory study.* Tripoli: Arab Development Institute, 1979.

Austin, Michel. "The Greeks in Libya." In *Greek Colonization* (2nd ed.). Edited by Gocha R. Tsetskhladze. Leiden, Nehterlands: Brill, 2008.

Bahgat, Gawdat. *Proliferation of nuclear weapons in the Middle East.* Gainesville: University Press of Florida, 2007.

Baker, Thomas. *Piracy and diplomacy in seventeenth-century North Africa: The journal of Thomas Baker, English consul in Tripoli, 1677–1685.* Edited with an introduction by C. R. Pennell. Rutherford, New Jersey: Fairleigh Dickinson University Press; London: Associated University Presses, 1989.

Baldinetti, Anna. "Italian Colonial Rule and the Muslim Elites in Libya: A Relationship of Antagonism and Collaboration." In *Guardians of Faith in Modern Times: Ulama' in the Middle East.* Edited by Meir Hatina. Leiden: Brill, 2008.

Barbar, Aghil M. *Government and politics in Libya, 1969–1978: A bibliography.* Monticello, IL: Vance Bibliographies, 1979.

Barclay, C. N. *Against great odds; the story of the first offensive in Libya in 1940–41, the first British victory in the Second World War; including many extracts from the personal account of Sir Richard N. O'Connor, and with a foreword by Sir John Harding.* London: Sifton, Praed, 1955.

Barker, Graeme et al. *Farming the desert: The UNESCO Libyan Valleys Archaeological Survey.* Paris: UNESCO Pub.; Tripoli: Department of Antiquities, Socialist People's Libyan Arab Jamahiriya; London: Society for Libyan Studies, 1996.

Barthel, Günter and Lothar Rathmann. *Libya: History, experiences and perspectives of a revolution.* Berlin: Akademie-Verlag, 1980.

Barton, Len. *Policy, experience and change: Cross- cultural reflections on inclusive education.* Dordrecht, Netherlands: Springer, 2008.

Battistelli, Pier Paolo. *Italian Blackshirt 1935–45.* Oxford: Osprey Publishing Ltd., 2010.

Bearman, Jonathan. *Qadhafi's Libya.* London;: Zed Books, 1986.

Behnke, Roy H. *The herders of Cyrenaica: Ecology, economy, and kinship among the Bedouin of eastern Libya.* Urbana: University of Illinois Press, 1980.

Bender, Gerald J., ed. *International affairs in Africa.* Newbury Park, CA: Sage Publications, 1987.

Bentham, Jeremy. *Securities against misrule and other constitutional writings for Tripoli and Greece.* (Philip Schofield, Ed.). New York: Oxford University Press, 1990.

Bianco, Mirella. *Gadafi: Voice from the desert*. Translated by Margaret Lyle. [*Kadhafi: messager du desert.*] London: Longman, 1975.

Bills, Scott L. *The Libyan arena: The United States, Britain, and the Council of Foreign Ministers, 1945–1948*. Kent, OH: Kent State University Press, 1995.

Blas de Roblès, Jean-Marie. *Libye grecque, romaine et byzantine*. (New ed.). Aix-en-Provence, France: Edisud, 2005.

Blundy, David and Andrew Lycett. *Qaddafi and the Libyan revolution*. London: Weidenfeld and Nicolson, 1987.

Bogin, Meg. *The women troubadours*. Scarborough, England: Paddington, 1976.

Brant, E. D. *Railways of North Africa: The railway system of the Maghreb: Algeria, Tunisia, Morocco and Libya*. Newton Abbot, England: David and Charles, 1971.

Braun, Ethel. *The new Tripoli and what I saw in the hinterland*. London: Darf, 1986.

Brill, M. *Libya*. Chicago: Children's Press, 1987.

Buck, D. J. and D. J Mattingly, eds. *Town and country in Roman Tripolitania: Papers in honour of Olwen*. Oxford: B.A.R., 1985.

Burgis, Michelle L. *Boundaries of discourse in the International Court of Justice: mapping arguments in Arab territorial disputes*. Boston: Martinus Nijhoff Publishers, 2009.

Buru, M. M., S. M. Ghanem, and K. S. McLachlan. *Planning and development in modern Libya*. London: Society for Libyan Studies, 1985.

Calderón, Horacio. *Khaddafi, la Operación "Jerusalén."* Buenos Aires, Argentina: Editorial Legión, 1981.

Campbell, Dugald. *Camels through Libya: A desert adventure from the fringes of the Sahara to the oases of Upper Egypt*. Philadelphia: J. B. Lippincott Co., 1935.

Caravelli, Jack. *Beyond sand and oil: The nuclear Middle East*. Westport: ABC-CLIO, 2011.

Carlson, Dennis. "Life among the Ruins of Empire: A Peace Corps Education in Libya." In *Examining social theory: Crossing borders/reflecting back*. Edited by Daniel Ethan Chapman. New York: P. Lang, 2010.

Carver, Michael. *Dilemmas of the desert war: A new look at the Libyan campaign, 1940–1942*. Bloomington: Indiana University Press, 1986.

Cheng, Tan Wee. *Hotspots and dodgy places: Travels through North Korea, Sudan and Distant Lands*. Singapore: Marshall Cavendish International (Asia) Ptd. Ltd., 2010.

Cholmeley-Eversheds, Frere. *Libya: A guide to commercial law, banking law and accounting*. London: GMB Publishing Ltd, 2008.

Collins, Catherine and Douglas Frantz. *Fallout: The true story of the CIA's secret war on nuclear trafficking*. New York: Free Press, 2011.

Cooley, John K. *Libyan sandstorm*. New York: Holt, Rinehart, and Winston, 1982.

Copeland, W. Paul. *The land and people of Libya*. New York: J. B. Lippincott, 1967.

Corera, Gordon. *Shopping for bombs: Nuclear proliferation, global insecurity, and the rise and fall of the A.Q. Khan Network*. New York: Oxford University Press, 2006.

Cortright, David. *The sanctions decade: Assessing U.N. strategies in the 1990s.* Boulder, CO: Lynne Rienner Publishers, 2000.

CQ Press. *Constitutions of the World.* Washington, DC: CQ Press, a Division of SAGE, 2007.

Davidson, Frank P. and Kathleen Lusk Brooke. *Building the world: An encyclopedia of the great engineering projects in history.* Westport, CT: Greenwood Press, 2006.

Davis, J. *Libyan politics: Tribe and revolution: An account of the Zuwaya and their government.* London: Tauris, 1987.

De Candole, E. A. V. *Life and times of King Idris of Libya.* London: E. A. V. De Candole, 1988.

Declaration on the establishment of the authority of the people in the Libyan Arab Republic. Washington, DC: Embassy of the Libyan Arab Republic, 1976.

Deeb, Marius and Mary Jane Deeb. *Libya since the revolution: Aspects of social and political development.* New York: Praeger, 1982.

De Felice, Renzo. *Jews in an Arab land: Libya, 1835–1970.* Transl. Judith Roumani. Austin: University of Texas Press, 1985.

Deif, Farida. *Libya: A threat to society?: The arbitrary detention of women and girls for "social rehabilitation."* New York: Human Rights Watch, 2006.

Del Boca, Angelo. *Mohamed Fekini and the Fight to Free Libya.* Basingstoke: Palgrave Macmillan, 2011.

Di Vita, Antonino. *Libya: The lost cities of the Roman Empire.* Cologne, Germany: Könemann, 1999.

Drachman, Edward R. *Presidents and foreign policy: Countdown to ten controversial decisions.* Albany: State University of New York Press, 1997.

Dwyer, Daisy Hilse (Ed.). *Law and Islam in the Middle East* New York: Bergin and Garvey Publishers, 1990.

El-Ghonemy, M. Riad. *Anti-poverty land reform issues never die: Collected essays on development economics in practice.* Hoboken, NJ: Taylor and Francis, 2009.

Elkaddi, Ibrahim Mohamed. *Housing in Libya: An analysis of conditions and a proposal for housing-service organization based on the neighborhood unit concept.* Austin, TX: 1978.

El-Khawas, Mohamed A. *Qaddafi: His ideology in theory and practice.* Brattleboro, VT: Amana Books, 1986.

El-Kikhia, Mansour O. *Libya's Qaddafi: The politics of contradiction.* Gainesville: University Press of Florida, 1997.

El Saadany, Salah. *Egypt and Libya from inside, 1969–1976: The Qaddafi revolution and the eventual break in relations.* Jefferson, NC: McFarland, 1994.

ElWarfally, Mahmoud G. *Imagery and ideology in U.S. policy toward Libya, 1969–1982.* Pittsburgh: University of Pittsburgh Press, 1988.

Entman, Robert M. *Projections of power: Framing news, public opinion, and U.S. foreign policy.* Chicago: The University of Chicago Press, 2004.

Esso Standard Libya. *Birth of an industry.* Malta: Author, 1969.

Esso Standard Libya. *The first billion barrels: Esso Libya (1954–1968)*. Libya: Author, 1968.

Esso Standard Libya. *The Islamic Heritage*. Tripoli: Author, 1970.

Faath, Sigrid (Ed.). *Anti-Americanism in the Islamic world*. London: Hurst, 2006.

Farmer, Henry George. *Historical facts for the Arabian musical influence*. North Stratford, NH: Ayer Publishing, 1978.

Faṭḥalī, Umar Ibrāhiīm and Monte Palmer. *Political development and social change in Libya*. Lexington, MA: Lexington Books, 1980.

Field, Ophelia. *Libya: Stemming the flow: Abuses against migrants, asylum seekers and refugees*. New York: Human Rights Watch, 2006.

First, Ruth. *Libya: The elusive revolution*. New York: Africana Pub. Co., 1975.

Fleagle, John G. et al. *Elwyn Simons: A search for origins*. New York: Springer, 2008.

Ford, Ken. *Operation Crusader 1941: Rommel in Retreat*. Oxford: Osprey Publishing Ltd., 2010.

Frelick, Bill. *Pushed back, pushed around: Italy's forced return of boat migrants and asylum seekers, Libya's mistreatment of migrants and asylum seekers*. New York: Human Rights Watch, 2009.

Galaty, Michael L. *Archaeology under dictatorship*. Dordrecht: Springer, 2006.

Geldenhuys, D. *Deviant conduct in world politics*. New York: Palgrave Macmillan, 2004.

Georgy, Guy. *Kadhafi, le berger des Syrtes: Pages d'éphéméride*. Paris: Flammarion, 1996.

Goldberg, Harvey E. *Cave dwellers and citrus growers: A Jewish community in Libya and Israel*. Cambridge, University Press, 1972.

Goldberg, Harvey E. *Jewish life in Muslim Libya: Rivals and relatives*. Chicago: University of Chicago Press, 1990.

Gottfried, Ted. *Libya: Desert land in conflict*. Brookfield, CT: Millbrook Press, 1994.

Goudarzi, Gus Hossein. *A summary of the geologic history of Libya*. Washington, DC: U.S. Geological Survey, 1959.

Goulden, Joseph C. and Alexander W. Raffio. *The death merchant: The rise and fall of Edwin P. Wilson*. London: Sidgwick and Jackson, 1985.

Great Britain Commercial Relations and Exports Department. *Libya: Economic and commercial conditions in Libya*. London: Published for the Board of Trade, Commercial Relations and Exports Department, by H. M. Stationery Office, 1952.

Great Britain Naval Intelligence Division. *A handbook of Libya*. Compiled by the Geographical section of the Naval Intelligence division, Naval staff, Admiralty. London: H. M. Stationery Office, 1920.

Great Britain Foreign Office Historical Section. *Italian Libya*. London: H. M. Stationery Office, 1920.

Great Britain War Office. *Destruction of an army: The first campaign in Libya: Sept. 1940–Feb. 1941*. London: H. M. Stationery Office, 1941.

Green World Institute. *Le Procès de Reagan: Après les bombardements U.S. de Tripoli et de Benghazi*. Paris: L'Harmattan, 1990.

Guderzo, Max. *The Globalization of the Cold War: Diplomacy and local confrontation, 1975–1985.* Hoboken, NJ: Taylor and Francis, 2009.

Haass, Richard N. (Ed.). *Transatlantic tensions: The United States, Europe, and problem countries.* Washington, DC: Brookings Institution Press, 1999.

Haass, Richard N., (Ed.). *Economic sanctions and American diplomacy.* New York: Council on Foreign Relations, 1998.

Haley, P. Edward. *Qaddafi and the United States since 1969.* New York: Praeger, 1984.

Hammond Incorporated. *Middle East crisis.* Maplewood, NJ: Author, 1990.

Hamza, Mohamed Hameda. *Rapid growth and urban transportation problems: A case study of Tripoli, Libya.* Austin, TX: University of Texas Press, 1979.

Harris, Lillian Craig. *Libya: Qadhafi's revolution and the modern state.* Boulder, CO: Westview Press; 1986.

Hassan, S. S. and M. M. Ali. "Migration Streams in Libya, 1954–64" In *Urbanization and migration in some Arab and African countries.* Cairo: Cairo Demographic Centre, 1973.

Henry, Clement M. and Robert Springborg (2nd ed.). *Globalization and the politics of development in the Middle East.* New York: Cambridge University Press, 2010.

Herbert, Edwin. *Risings and Rebellions, 1919–39: Interwar colonial campaigns in Africa, Asia, and the Americas.* Nottingham, UK: Foundry Books, 2007.

Hinnebusch, Raymond and Anoushiravan Ehteshami. *The foreign policies of Middle East states.* Boulder, CO: Lynne Rienner Publishers, 2002.

Hoyos, Dexter. *Truceless war: Carthage's fight for survival, 241 to 237 BC.* Leiden, Netherlands: Brill, 2007.

Human Rights Watch. *World Report 2008.* New York: Seven Stories Press, 2010.

Hurd, Ian. *After anarchy: Legitimacy and power in the United Nations Security.* Princeton, NJ: Princeton University Press, 2007.

Huskinson, Janet. *Roman sculpture from Cyrenaica in the British Museum.* London: British Museum Publications Ltd., 1975.

Joffé, E. G. H. and K. S. McLachlan. *Social and economic development of Libya.* Wisbech, Cambridgeshire, UK: Middle East and North African Studies Press, 1982.

Kaldor, Mary and Paul Anderson. *Mad dogs: The U.S. raids on Libya.* London: Pluto in association with European Nuclear Disarmament, 1986.

Katzman, Kenneth. *The Iran-Libya Sanctions Act (ILSA)* [microform]. Washington, DC: Congressional Research Service, Library of Congress, 2003.

Kelly, Sanja. *Women's rights in the Middle East and North Africa: Progress amid resistance.* Lanham: Rowman and Littlefield Publishing Group, Inc., 2010.

Kessler, Scott Jacob. *Deconstructing and reassembling the politics of American foreign policy: The U.S., Libya and Syria, 1980–1988.* Thesis (Ph. D.), University of Texas at Austin, 1991.

Khader, Bichara and Bashir El-Wifati. *The economic development of Libya.* Dover, N.H.: Croom Helm, 1987.

Khadduri, Majid. *Modern Libya: A study in political development.* Baltimore, Johns Hopkins Press, 1963.

Khalidi, Ismail Raghib. *Constitutional development in Libya.* Beirut, Lebanon: Khayat's College Book Cooperative, 1956.

Khazzoom Loolwa. *The flying camel: Essays on identity by women of North African and Middle Eastern Jewish heritage.* New York: Seal Press; [Emeryville, CA]: Publishers Group West, 2003.

Laham, Nicholas. *The American bombing of Libya: A study of the force of miscalculation in Reagan foreign policy.* Jefferson, NC: McFarland and Co., 2008.

Lawless, Richard I. *Libya.* Santa Barbara, CA: Clio, 1987.

Layish, Aharon. *Sharīa and custom in Libyan tribal society: An annotated translation of decisions from the Sharīa courts of Adjābiya.* With a linguistic essay by Alexander Borg. Boston: Brill, 2005.

Lemarchand, René. *The green and the glack: Qadhafi's policies in Africa.* Bloomington: Indiana University Press, 1988.

Le Tourneau, Roger. *Report of the mission to Libya.* Paris: United Nations Educational, Scientific and Cultural Organization, 1952.

Libya under Qadhafi: A pattern of aggression. Washington, DC: U.S. Department of State, Bureau of Public Affairs, 1986.

Lin, Connie. *Libya: A second opportunity for the oil and gas industry.* Thesis (M.A.), University of Texas at Austin, 2005.

Little, Douglas. *American Orientalism: The United States and the Middle East since 1945* (3rd ed.). Chapel Hill: University of North Carolina Press, 2008.

Litwak, Robert. *Regime change: U.S. strategy through the prism of 9/11.* Baltimore: Johns Hopkins University Press, 2007.

Maas, Peter. *Manhunt.* New York: Random House, 1986.

MacFarquhar, Neil. *The media relations department of Hizbollah wishes you a happy birthday: Unexpected encounters in the changing Middle East.* New York: Public Affairs, 2009.

Maqaryif, Muammad Yūsuf. *Coup led by an informer.* Uksfūrd, Libya: Markaz al-Dirāsāt al-Lībīyah, 2009.

Marghani, Amin B. D. *Ghibli: A study of the geography and politics of air transport in Libya and North Africa.* Cambridgeshire, UK: Middle East and North African Studies Press Ltd., 1991.

Martel, William C. *Victory in war: Foundations of modern military policy.* New York: Cambridge University Press, 2007.

Martínez, Luis. *The Libyan paradox.* transl. by John King. New York: Columbia University Press, 2007.

Mason, John P. *Island of the Blest: Islam in a Libyan oasis community.* Athens: Ohio University, Center for International Studies, 1977.

Matar, Hisham. *In the country of men.* London: Viking, 2006.

Matar, Khalil I. *Lockerbie and Libya: A study in international relations.* Jefferson, NC: McFarland and Co., 2004.

Mattingly, D. J. *Tripolitania.* London: B.T. Batsford, 1995.

May, Jacques M. *The ecology of malnutrition in Northern Africa: Libya, Tunisia, Algeria, Morocco, Spanish Sahara, and Ifni, Mauritania.* New York: Hafner Pub. Co., 1967.

Mayer, Ann Elizabeth. "Islamic Law and Islamic Revival in Libya," In *Islam in the Contemporary World.* Edited by Cyriac K. Pullapilly. Notre Dame, IN: Cross Roads Books, 1980.

McLaren, Brian. *Architecture and tourism in Italian colonial Libya: An ambivalent modernism.* Seattle: University of Washington Press, 2006.

McNamara, Thomas E. "Unilateral and Multilateral Strategies against State Sponsors of Terror: A Case Study of Libya, 1979 to 2003." In *Uniting against Terror: Cooperative Nonmilitary Responses to the Global Terrorist Threat.* Edited by David Cortright and George A. Lopez. Cambridge, MA: M.I.T. Press, 2007.

Menocal, María Rosa, Raymond P. Scheindlin, and Michael Anthony Sells (Eds.). *Cambridge history of Arabic literature.* Cambridge: Cambridge University Press, 2000.

Metz, Helen Chapin (Ed.) *Libya: A country study.* Washington, DC: Library of Congress, 1987.

Mewshaw, Michael. *Between terror and tourism: An overland journey across North Africa.* Berkeley, CA: Counterpoint, 2010.

Miller, Catherine et al. (Eds.). *Arabic in the city: Issues in dialect contact and language variation.* New York: Routledge, 2007.

Miller, Judith. *God has ninety-nine names: Reporting from a militant Middle East.* New York: Simon and Schuster, 1997.

Miller, Ward A. *The 9th Australian Division versus the Africa Corps: An infantry division against tanks: Tobruk, Libya, 1941.* Fort Leavenworth, KS: U.S. Army Command and General Staff College, Combat Studies Institute, 1986.

Mitcham, Samuel W. *Rommel's greatest victory: The Desert Fox and the fall of Tobruk, spring 1942.* Novato, CA: Presidio Press, 1998.

Monti-Belkaoui, Janice. *Qaddafi: The man and his policies.* Brookfield, VT: Ashgate Pub. Co., 1996.

Morayef, Heba. *Truth and justice can't wait: Human rights developments in Libya amid institutional obstacles.* New York: Human Rights Watch, 2009.

Mueller, Andrew. *I wouldn't start from here: The 21st century and where it all went wrong.* Brooklyn: Soft Skull, 2007.

Myers, Robert J. (Ed.). *Religion and the state: The struggle for legitimacy and power.* Beverly Hills, CA: Sage Publications, 1986.

Nafziger, James A. R. and Ann M. Nicgorski (Eds.). *Cultural heritage issues: The legacy of conquest, colonization, and commerce.* Leiden [The Netherlands]: Martinus Nijhoff Publishers, 2009.

Najem, Tom Pierre. "State Power and Democratization in North Africa: Developments in Morocco, Algeria, Tunisia, and Libya." In *Democratization in the Middle East: Experiences, struggles, challenges.* Edited by Amin Saikal and Albrecht Schnabel. Tokyo: United Nations University Press, 2003.

Narbrough, John, Sir [Admiral of His Majesties fleet in the Mediterranean, on the 14th of January, 1675/6; together with an account of his taking afterwards five barks laden with corn, and of his farther action on that coast]. *A particular narrative of the burning in the port of Tripoli, four men of war, belonging to those corsairs* [microform]. London: In the Savoy, Tho. Newcomb, 1676.

Naylor, Phillip Chiviges. *North Africa: A history from antiquity to the present.* Austin: University of Texas Press, 2009.

Nelson, Harold D. *Libya: A country study* (3rd ed.). Washington, DC: The University: U.S. Government Printing Office, 1979.

Neuberger, Ralph Benyamin. *Involvement, invasion and withdrawal: Qadhdhāfi's Libya and Chad, 1969–1981.* Tel-Aviv: Tel-Aviv University, Shiloah Center for Middle Eastern and African Studies, 1982.

Newell, Clayton R. *Egypt-Libya.* Washington, DC: U.S. Army Center of Military History: U.S. Government Printing Office, 1993.

Niblock, Tim. *"Pariah states" and sanctions in the Middle East: Iraq, Libya, Sudan.* Boulder, CO: Lynne Rienner Publishers, 2001.

Nickerson, Jane Soames. *A short history of North Africa, from pre-Roman times to the present: Libya, Tunisia, Algeria, Morocco.* New York, Devin-Adair Co., 1961.

Nolutshungu, Sam C. *Limits of anarchy: Intervention and state formation in Chad.* Charlottesville: University Press of Virginia, 1996.

Norman, John. *Labor and politics in Libya and Arab Africa.* New York: Bookman Associates, 1965.

Obeidi, Amal. *Political culture in Libya.* Richmond, Surrey [England]: Curzon, 2001.

O'Sullivan, Meghan L. *Shrewd sanctions: Statecraft and state sponsors of terrorism.* Washington, DC: Brookings Institution Press, 2003.

Owens, Jonathan. *A short reference grammar of eastern Libyan Arabic.* Wiesbaden, Germany: O. Harrassowitz, 1984.

Paoletti, Emanuela. *The migration of power and north-south inequalities: The case of Italy and Libya.* Basingstoke, UK: Palgrave Macmillan, 2010.

Pasha, Aftab Kamal. *Libya in the Arab world: Qadhafi's quest for Arab unity.* Aligarh, India: Centre for West Asian Studies, Aligarh Muslim University, 1988.

Pasha, Aftab Kamal. *Libya and the United States: Qadhafi's response to Reagan's challenge.* New Delhi, India: Detente Publications, 1984.

PennWell Publishing Company. *Libya oil and gas: International petroleum encyclopedia.* Tulsa, OK: PennWell Corp., 2006.

People's Committee for Students of the Socialist People's Libyan Arab Jamahiriya. *Understanding Libya's role in world politics.* Washington, DC: Self Published, 1984.

Perdue, William. *Terrorism and the state: A critique of domination through fear.* Santa Barbara, CA: ABC-CLIO, 1989.

Peters, Emrys L. *The Bedouin of Cyrenaica: Studies in personal and corporate power.* New York: Cambridge University Press, 1990.

Petroleum Economist Ltd. *Energy map of Libya.* London: Petroleum Economist, 2008.

Pierce, Chris. *Corporate Governance in the Middle East and North Africa.* London: Blue Ibex Ltd., 2008.

Political handbook of the Middle East 2008. Washington, DC: CQ Press, 2008.

Pollack, Kenneth M. *Arabs at war: Military effectiveness, 1948–1991*. Lincoln: University of Nebraska Press, 2004.

Putzi, Sibylla. *A to Z world lifecycles: 175 countries: birth, childhood, coming of age, dating and courtship, marriage, family and parenting, work life, old age and death*. Petaluma, California: World Trade Press, 2008.

Putzi, Sibylla. *A to Z world religion: 175 countries: religions of the country, basic tenets, religious conflict, secularism, superstitions, religious clerics, and more*. Petaluma, California: World Trade Press, 2008.

Putzi, Sibylla. *A to Z world superstitions and folklore: 175 countries: spirit worship, curses, mystical characters, folk tales, burial and the dead, animals, food, marriage, good luck, and more*. Petaluma, california: World Trade Press, 2008.

Qaddafi, Muammar. *Qaddafi's Green Book* (an unauthorized ed.). Edited by Henry M. Christman. Buffalo, NY: Prometheus Books, 1988.

Qaddafi, Muammar. (M. Al Gathafi). *The green book: The solution to the problem of democracy, the solution to the economic problem, the social basis of the third universal theory*. Reading, England: Ithaca Press, 2005.

Qaddafi, Muammar. *The green book* (10th ed.). Tripoli: World Center for Studies and Research of the Green Book, 1987.

Ranjit Kaur. *Islamic co-operation and unity: Socio-political, economic and military relations with special reference to Pakistan, Libya, and Sudan*. New Delhi: Deep and Deep Publications, 1993.

Reich, Bernard. *Handbook of political science research on the Middle East and North Africa*. Westport, CT: Greenwood Press, 1998.

Richter, Lore. *Islands of the Sahara: through the oases of Libya*. [English translation by Hermann Ehlert]. Leipzig: Edition Leipzig, 1960.

The road to people's authority: A collection of historical speeches and documents. Libya: The Information Section, The People's Committee for Students of the Socialist People's Libyan Arab Jamahiriya, 1980.

Robertson, Noel. *Religion and reconciliation in Greek cities: The sacred laws of Selinus and Cyrene*.New York: Oxford University Press, 2010.

Rolls, S. C. *Steel chariots in the desert: The story of an armoured-car driver with the Duke of Westminster in Libya and in Arabia with T. E. Lawrence*. London: J. Cape, 1937.

Ronen, Yehudit. *Qaddafi's Libya in world politics*. Boulder, CO: Lynne Rienner Publishers, 2008.

Roumani, Maurice M. *The Jews of Libya: Coexistence, persecution, resettlement*. Portland, OR: Sussex Academic Press, 2008.

Rugh, William A. *Arab mass media: Newspapers, radio, and television in Arab politics*. Santa Barbara, CA: ABC-CLIO, 2004.

Saikal, Amin and Albrecht Schnabel. *Democratization in the Middle East: Experiences, struggles, challenges*. New York: United Nations University Press, 2003.

Sam, Nolutshungu C. *Limits of anarchy: Intervention and state formation in Chad*. Charlottesville: University Press of Virginia, 1996.

Segrè, Claudio G. *Fourth shore: The Italian colonization of Libya*. Chicago: University of Chicago Press, 1974.

Sicker, Martin. *The making of a pariah state: The adventurist politics of Muammar Qaddafi*. New York: Praeger, 1987.

Siddiqui, Kalim. *Towards a new destiny*. London: Newsmedia Book Service, 1974.

Simon, Rachel. *Change within tradition among Jewish women in Libya*. Seattle: University of Washington Press, 1992.

Simpson, G. E. *The heart of Libya: The Siwa Oasis, its people, customs and sport*. London: H. F. and G. Witherby, 1929.

Sono, Themba. *Libya: The vilified revolution*. Langley Park, MD: Progress Press Publications, 1984.

Sorenson, David S. *An introduction to the modern Middle East: History, religion, political economy, politics*. Boulder, CO: Westview Press, 2008.

Stanik, Joseph T. *El Dorado Canyon: Reagan's undeclared war with Qaddafi*. Annapolis, MD: Naval Institute Press, 2003.

Stanik, Joseph T. *Swift and effective retribution: The U.S. Sixth Fleet and the confrontation with Qaddafi*. Washington, DC: Naval Historical Center, Department of the Navy, U.S. Government Printing Office, 1996.

Stanley, Sadie and John Tyrr (Eds.). *Grove dictionary of music and musicians*. London: Macmillan Press.

Stillman, Yedida and Norman A Stillman. *From Iberia to diaspora: Studies in Sephardic history and culture*. Boston: Brill, 1999.

St. John, Ronald Bruce. *Libya: Continuity and change*. Abingdon, Oxon; New York: Routledge, 2011.

St. John, Ronald Bruce. *Libya: from colony to independence*. Oxford: Oneworld, 2008.

St. John, Ronald Bruce. *Libya and the United States: Two centuries of strife*. Philadelphia: University of Pennsylvania Press, 2002.

St. John, Ronald Bruce. Historical dictionary of Libya (3rd ed.). Lanham, MD: Scarecrow Press, 1998.

St. John, Ronald Bruce. *Qaddafi's world design: Libyan foreign policy, 1969–1987*. Atlantic Highlands, NJ: Saqi Books, 1987.

Summary of Amnesty International's prisoner concerns in the Great Socialist People's Libyan Arab Jamahiriya. New York: Amnesty International, National Office, 1987.

Teebi, Ahmad S. *Genetic disorders among Arab populations* (2nd ed.). Dordrecht, The Netherlands: Springer, 2010.

Thiry, Jacques. *Le Sahara libyen dans l'Afrique du nord medieval*. Leuven, Belgium: Departement Oosterse Studies, 1995.

Thwaite, Anthony. *The deserts of Hesperides: An experience of Libya*. London: Secker and Warburg, 1969.

Trend, J. B. *Music of Spanish history to 1600*. New York: Krause, 1965.

Tully, Miss. *Letters written during a ten years' residence at the court of Tripoli, 1783–1795: Published from the originals in the possession of the family of the late Richard Tully, esq., the British Consul: Comprising authentic memoirs and anecdotes of the reigning Bashaw, his family, and other persons of distinction. Also an account of the domestic manners of the Moors, Arabs and Turks; with a new introduction by Caroline Stone* (new ed.). Kilkerran, UK: Hardinge Simpole, 2009.

U.S. Congress: Senate Committee on Government Operations. *Report of a study of United States foreign aid in ten Middle Eastern and African countries: Turkey, Iran, Syria, Lebanon, Jordan, Israel, Greece, Tunisia, Libya, Egypt.* Submitted by Ernest Gruening, Subcommittee on Reorganization and International Organization of the Committee on Government Operations, United States Senate. Washington, DC: U.S. Government Printing Office, 1963.

U.S. Congress: Senate Committee on Banking, Housing, and Urban Affairs. *Reauthorization of the Iran-Libya Sanctions Act: Hearing before the Committee on Banking, Housing, and Urban Affairs, United States Senate, One Hundred Ninth Congress, second session, on reauthorization of the Iran-Libya Sanctions Act in relation to the security of the Middle East region, June 22, 2006.* Washington, DC: U.S. Government Printing Office, 2006.

U.S. Congress: House Committee on International Relations. Subcommittee on the Middle East and Central Asia. *Enforcement of the Iran-Libya Sanctions Act and increasing security threats from Iran: Hearing before the Subcommittee on the Middle East and Central Asia of the Committee on International Relations, House of Representatives, One Hundred Eighth Congress, first session, June 25, 2000:* Enforcement of the Iran Libya Sanctions Act and increasing security threats from Iran. Washington, DC: U.S. Government Printing Office, 2003.

U.S. Congress: House Committee on Foreign Affairs. Subcommittee on International Economic Policy and Trade. *Sanctions against Libya: Hearing and markup before the Committee on Foreign Affairs and its Subcommittee on International Economic Policy and Trade, House of Representatives, Ninety-ninth Congress, second session on H.R. 4847, May 20 and June 5, 1986.* Washington, DC: U.S. Government Printing Office, 1988.

U.S. Congress: House Committee on International Relations. Subcommittee on Africa. *U.S. Libya relations: A new era?: Hearing before the Subcommittee on Africa of the Committee on International Relations, House of Representatives, One Hundred Sixth Congress, first session, Tuesday, July 22, 1999: U.S. Libya relations.* Washington, DC: U.S. Government Printing Office, 2000.

U.S. Congress: Senate Committee on Foreign Relations. Subcommittee on Near Eastern and South Asian Affairs. *U.S. foreign policy toward Libya: Hearing before the Subcommittee on Near Eastern and South Asian Affairs of the Committee on Foreign Relations, United States Senate, One Hundred Sixth Congress, second session, May 4, 2000: U.S. foreign policy toward Libya.* Washington, DC: U.S. Government Printing Office, 2000.

U.S. Congress: House Committee on International Relations. *Libya: Progress on the path toward cautious reengagement: Hearing before the Committee on International Relations, House of Representatives, One Hundred Ninth Congress, first session, March 16, 2005.* Washington, DC: U.S. Government Printing Office, 2005.

U.S. Congress: House Committee on International Relations. Subcommittee on Europe. *Calling on government of Libya to review legal actions taken against Bulgarian medical workers, urging the President of the E.U. to add Hezbollah to E.U.'s wide-ranging list of terrorist organizations, pledging continued U.S. support for the Republic of Georgia, congratulating Serbia for conducting a democratic, free and fair presidential election and for reaffirming Serbia's commitment to peace, democracy and the rule of law, relating to the reunification of Cyprus: markup before the Subcommittee on Europe of the Committee on International Relations, House of Representatives, One Hundred Eighth Congress, second session on H. Res. 733, H. Res. 341, H. Res. 483, H. Res. 726 and H. Con Res. 412, October 5, 2004.*Washington, DC: U.S. Government Printing Office, 2004.

U.S. Congress: Senate Committee on Foreign Relations. *Libya, next steps in U.S. relations: Hearing before the Committee on Foreign Relations, United Senate, One Hundred Eighth Congress, second session, February 26, 2004.* Washington, DC: U.S. Government Printing Office, 2004.

U.S. Congress: House Committee on International Relations. Subcommittee on International Terrorism, Nonproliferation, and Human Rights. *Disarmament of Libya's weapons of mass destruction: Hearing before the Subcommittee on International Terrorism, Nonproliferation and Human Rights of the Committee on International Relations, House of Representatives, One Hundred Eighth Congress, second session, September 22, 2004.* Washington, DC: U.S. Government Printing Office, 2004.

U.S. Central Intelligence Agency. *Libya.* Washington, DC: Author, 1993.

U.S. Central Intelligence Agency. *The Middle East.* Washington, DC: Author, 1990.

U.S. Department of Energy. *The petroleum resources of Libya, Algeria, and Egypt.* Washington, DC: Energy Information Administration, Office of Oil and Gas, U.S. Department of Energy: U.S. Government Printing Office, 1984.

U.S. Department of Information and Cultural Affairs. *The human march in the Libyan Arab Republic.* Washington, DC: Author, 1976.

U.S. Department of State Bureau of Public Affairs. *The Libyan problem: October 1983.* Washington, DC: Author, 1983.

U.S. Geological Survey. *U.S. Geological Survey assessment of undiscovered petroleum resources of the Hamra Basin, Libya, 2006.* Reston, VA: U.S. Department of the Interior, U.S. Geological Survey, 2007.

Vandewalle, Dirk. *Libya since 1969: Qadhafi's revolution revisited.* New York: Palgrave Macmillan, 2008.

Vandewalle, Dirk. *A history of modern Libya.*New York: Cambridge University Press, 2006.

Vandewalle, Dirk. *Libya since independence: Oil and state-building.* Ithaca, NY: Cornell University Press, 1998.

Vandewalle, Dirk. *Qadhafi's Libya, 1969–1994.* New York: St. Martin's Press, 1995.

Villard, Henry Serrano. *Libya: The new Arab kingdom of North Africa.* Ithaca, NY: Cornell University Press, 1956.

Waddams, Frank C. *The Libyan oil industry.* Baltimore: Johns Hopkins University Press, 1980.

Ward, Philip. *Touring Libya: The southern provinces.* London: Faber, 1968.

Whitehead, Don. *Combat reporter: Don Whitehead's World War II diary and memoirs.* Edited by John B. Romeiser. New York: Fordham University Press, 2006.

Wiegele, Thomas C. *The clandestine building of Libya's chemical weapons factory: A study in international collusion.* Carbondale, IL: Southern Illinois University Press, 1992.

Winn, Neil. *European crisis management in the 1980s.* Brookfield, VT: Dartmouth, 1996.

Wisdom, T. H. *"Wings over Olympus": The story of the Royal Air Force in Libya and Greece.* London: G. Allen and Unwin Ltd., 1942.

Wizārat Shu'un al-Batrūl. *Petroleum development in Libya, 1954 through mid 1963.* Tripoli: Ministry of Public Affairs, 1963.

Woodard, Aleen. *Sand in my shoes.* Austin, TX: Nortex Press, 1985.

Words without Borders. *Literature from the "Axis of Evil": Writing from Iran, Iraq, North Korea, and other enemy nations.* New York: New Press, 2007.

World Trade Press. *Libya media, internet and telecommunications complete profile: This all-inclusive profile includes all three of our communications reports* (2nd ed.). Petaluma, California: Author, 2010.

World Trade Press. *Libya money and banking: The basics on currency and money in Libya* (2nd ed.). Petaluma, California: Author, 2010.

World Trade Press. *Libya society and culture complete report: An all-inclusive profile combining all of our society and culture reports* (2nd ed.). Petaluma, California: Author, 2010.

World Trade Press. *Libya travel complete profile: The all-inclusive travel report for Libya* (2nd ed.). Petaluma, California: Author, 2010.

World Trade Press. *Libya women in culture, business and travel: A profile of Libyan women in the fabric of society* (2nd ed.). Petaluma, California: Author, 2010.

Wright, Claudia. *The politics of liquidation: The Reagan administration policy toward the Arabs.* Belmont, MA: Association of Arab-American University Graduates, 1986.

Wright, John L. *Libya: A modern history.* Baltimore, MD: Johns Hopkins University Press, 1982.

Wright, John L. *Libya, Chad and the central Sahara.* London: Hurst, 1989.

Yankah, Kojo. *End of a journey, or, a journalist's report from the Libyan Jamahiriya,* with an introduction by Atukwei Okai. Accra, Ghana: Dateline, 1984.

Zartman, I. William, Mark A. Tessler, John P. Entells, Russell A. Stone, Raymond A. Hinnebusch, and Sharrough Akhavi. *Political elites in Arab North Africa: Morocco, Algeria, Tunisia, Libya, and Egypt.* New York: Longman, 1982.

Ziadeh, Farhat Jacob. *Property law in the Arab world: Real rights in Egypt, Iraq, Jordan, Lebanon, Libya, Syria, Saudi Arabia, and the Gulf States.* London: Graham and Trotman, 1979.

Zoubir, Yahia H. and Haizam Amirah-Fernández. *North Africa: Politics, region, and the limits of transformation.*New York: Routledge, 2008.

ARTICLES

Ahmida, Ali Abdullatif. "Forgotten Voices: Power and Agency in Colonial and Postcolonial Libya." *Middle East Journal* Vol. 60, No. 3 (Summer 2006): 588–589.

Alexander, Nathan. "Libya: The Continuous Revolution." *Middle Eastern Studies* Vol. 17, No. 2 (Apr. 1981): 210–227.

Allan, J. A. and K. S. McLachlan. "Agricultural Development in Libya after Oil." *African Affairs* Vol. 75, No. 300 (Jul. 1976): 331–348.

Anderson, Lisa. "Religion and State in Libya: The Politics of Identity." *Annals of the American Academy of Political and Social Science* Vol. 483 (Jan., 1986): 61–72.

Anderson, Lisa. "Libya and American Foreign Policy." *Middle East Journal* Vol. 36, No. 4 (Autumn 1982): 516–534.

Anderson, Lisa. "Rogue Libya's Long Road." *Middle East Report* No. 241, *Iran: Looking Ahead* (Winter 2006): 42–47.

Anderson, Lisa. "Nineteenth-Century Reform in Ottoman Libya." *International Journal of Middle East Studies* Vol. 16, No. 3 (Aug., 1984): 325–348.

Austin, Granville. "The Libya Raid and the Arab-Israel Dispute." *Journal of Palestine Studies*, Vol. 15, No. 4 (Summer 1986): 99–111.

Blackwell, Stephen. "Saving the King: Anglo-American Strategy and British Counter-Subversion Operations in Libya, 1953–59." *Middle Eastern Studies* Vol. 39, No. 1 (Jan. 2003): 1–18.

Blowers, G. A. and A. N. McLeod. "Currency Unification in Libya." *Staff Papers- International Monetary Fund.* Vol. 2, No. 3 (Nov. 1952): 439–467.

Boardman, J. "Excavations at Tocra in Libya, 1964–66." *Archaeological Reports* No. 12 (1965–1966): 25–26.

Bovill, E. W. "Italy in Africa: Part II." *Journal of the Royal African Society* Vol. 32, No. 129 (Oct. 1933): 350–361.

Brailsford, H. N. "Impressions of Tunis and Libya." *International Affairs (Royal Institute of International Affairs 1931–1939)* Vol. 18, No. 3 (May–June 1939): 361–379.

Buera, Abu and William Glueck. "Stage of Economic Development and the Managerial Elite: The Case of Libya." *Management International Review* Vol. 18, No. 1 (1978): 33–42.

Buis, Georges and Laila Ghanem. "Georges Buis: Terrorism and the U.S. Libya Raid." *Journal of Palestine Studies* Vol. 15, No. 4 (Summer 1986): 112–119.

Carey, Jane Perry Clark and Andrew Galbraith Carey. "Libya: No Longer 'Arid Nurse of Lions.' " *Political Science Quarterly* Vol. 76, No. 1 (Mar. 1961): 47–68.

Carvely, Andrew. "Libya: International Relations and Political Purposes." *International Journal* Vol. 28, No. 4, (Autumn 1973): 707–728.

Clarke, John I. "Oil in Libya: Some Implications." *Economic Geography* Vol. 39, No. 1 (Jan. 1963): 40–59.

Collins, Carole. "Imperialism and Revolution in Libya." *MERIP Reports* No. 27 (Apr. 1974): 3–22.

Cordell, Dennis D. "The Awlad Sulayman of Libya and Chad: Power and Adaptation in the Sahara and Sahel." *Canadian Journal of African Studies/Revue Canadienne des Études Africaines* Vol. 19, No. 2 (1985): 319–343.

Cordell, Dennis D. "Eastern Libya, Wadai and the Sanūsīya: A arīqa and a Trade Route." *Journal of African History* Vol. 18, No. 1 (1977): 21–36.

Cunsolo, Ronald S. "Libya, Italian Nationalism, and the Revolt against Giolitti." *Journal of Modern History* Vol. 37, No. 2 (Jun. 1965): 186–207.

Daniels, Richard. "Creating a New Libya." *World Affairs* Vol. 114, No. 2 (Summer 1951): 47–49.

D. C. C. "The Nationalist Movement in Libya." *World Today* Vol. 2, No. 7 (Jul. 1946): 330–339.

Dearden, Ann. "Independence for Libya: The Political Problems." *Middle East Journal* Vol. 4, No. 4 (Oct. 1950): 395–409.

Deeb, Mary-Jane. "Libya's Foreign Policy in North Africa." *Middle East Journal* Vol. 45, No. 4 (Autumn 1991): 682–683.

Dupree, Louis. "The Non-Arab Ethnic Groups of Libya." *Middle East Journal* Vol. 12, No. 1 (Winter 1958): 33–44.

El Asswad, Rajab M. "Agricultural Prospects and Water Resources in Libya." *Ambio* Vol. 24, No. 6 (Sep. 1995): 324–327.

El Mallakh, Ragaei. "Affluence versus Development: Libya." *World Today* Vol. 24, No. 11 (Nov. 1968): 475–482.

El Mallakh, Ragaei. "The Economics of Rapid Growth: Libya." *Middle East Journal* Vol. 23, No. 3 (Summer 1969): 308–320.

Evans, Alona E. "*Bosco Middle East Oil Corp. v. Bank of America.* 343 F.Supp. 1072." *American Journal of International Law* Vol. 67, No. 1 (Jan. 1973): 152–153.

Fathaly, Omar I. and Monte Palmer. "Opposition to Change in Rural Libya Opposition to Change in Rural Libya." *International Journal of Middle East Studies* Vol. 11, No. 2 (Apr. 1980): 247–261.

Fisher, W. B. "Problems of Modern Libya." *Geographical Journal* Vol. 119, No. 2 (Jun. 1953): 183–195.

Fowler, Gary L. "Decolonization of Rural Libya." *Annals of the Association of American Geographers* Vol. 63, No. 4 (Dec. 1973): 490–506.

F. S. "Libya: Seven Years of Independence." *World Today* Vol. 15, No. 2 (Feb. 1959): 59–68.

Gohrbandt, K. H. A. "Some Cenomanian Foraminifera from Northwestern Libya." *Micropaleontology* Vol. 12, No. 1 (Jan. 1966): 65–70.

Goodchild, R. G. "Mapping Roman Libya." *Geographical Journal* Vol. 118, No. 2 (Jun. 1952): 142–152.

Harrison, Robert S. "Migrants in the City of Tripoli." *Geographical Review* Vol. 57, No. 3 (Jul. 1967): 397–423.

Heitmann, George. "Libya: An Analysis of the Oil Economy." *Journal of Modern African Studies* Vol. 7, No. 2 (Jul. 1969): 249–263.

Higgins, Benjamin. "Entrepreneurship in Libya." *Middle East Journal* Vol. 11, No. 3 (Summer 1957): 319–323.

Hinnebusch, Raymond A. "Charisma, Revolution, and State Formation: Qaddafi and Libya." *Third World Quarterly* Vol. 6, No. 1 (Jan., 1984): 59–73.

Huliaras, Asteris. "Qadhafi's Comeback: Libya and Sub-Saharan Africa in the 1990s." *African Affairs* Vol. 100, No. 398 (Jan. 2001): 5–25.

Hurd, Ian. "The Strategic Use of Liberal Internationalism: Libya and the U.N. Sanctions, 1992–2003." *International Organization* Vol. 59, No. 3 (Summer 2005): 495–526.

Ibrahim, Muhammad. "Libya: The Sons Also Rise." *Foreign Policy* No. 139 (Nov./Dec. 2003): 37–39.

"Italian Possessions in Africa: I." *Bulletin of International News* Vol. 17, No. 15 (Jul. 27, 1940): 925–929.

Jentleson, Bruce W. and Christopher A. Whytock. "Who 'Won' Libya?: The Force-Diplomacy Debate and Its Implications for Theory and Policy." *International Security* Vol. 30, No. 3 (Winter, 2005–2006): 47–86.

Joffe, George. "Islamic Opposition in Libya." *Third World Quarterly* Vol. 10, No. 2, *Islam and Politics* (Apr. 1988): 615–631.

Joffe, E. G. H. "Libya and Chad." *Review of African Political Economy* No. 21 (May–Sep. 1981): 84–102.

Kiernan, Bette Unger. "A Systems Perspective on Soviet-American Relations." *Political Psychology* Vol. 8, No. 2 (Jun. 1987): 245–247.

Kirkbride, Alec. "Libya: Which Way Facing?" *African Affairs* Vol. 56, No. 222 (Jan. 1957): 49–55.

Korczyn, A. D. "Creutzfeldt-Jakob Disease among Libyan Jews." *European Journal of Epidemiolog* Vol. 7, No. 5, Symposium on Human and Zoonotic Spongiform Encephalopathies (Sep. 1991): 490–493.

Kraeling, Carl H. "Now and Then in Libya." *Journal of the American Oriental Society* Vol. 80, No. 2 (Apr.–Jun. 1960): 104–111.

Leigh, Monroe. "*Libyan Arab Foreign Bank v. Bankers Trust Co.* 1986 L. Nos 1567, 4048. *Libyan Arab Foreign Bank v. Bankers Trust Co.* 1986 L. Nos 1567, 4048." *American Journal of International Law* Vol. 82, No. 1 (Jan. 1988): 132–136.

Lewis, William H. and Robert Gordon. "Libya after Two Years of Independence." *Middle East Journal* Vol. 8, No. 1 (Winter 1954): 41–53.

Mason, John Paul. "Oasis Saints of Eastern Libya in North African Context." *Middle Eastern Studies* Vol. 17, No. 3 (Jul. 1981): 357–374.

McDermott, Anthony. "Qaddafi and Libya." *World Today* Vol. 29, No. 9 (Sep. 1973): 398–408.

Mekie, D. E. C. "Appointments In Libya." *British Medical Journal* Vol. 2, No. 5708 (May 30, 1970): 544.

Moore, Clement Henry. "The Northeastern Triangle: Libya, Egypt, and the Sudan." *Annals of the American Academy of Political and Social Science* Vol. 489, *International Affairs in Africa* (Jan. 1987): 28–39.

Moore, Martin and Tracy Philipps. "Fourth Shore: Italy's Mass Colonisation of Libya." *Journal of the Royal African Society* Vol. 39, No. 155 (Apr. 1940): 129–133.

Oye, Ogunbadejo. "Qaddafi's North African Design." *International Security* Vol. 8, No. 1 (Summer): 154–178.

Pan, Chia-Lin. "The Population of Libya." *Population Studies* Vol. 3, No. 1 (Jun. 1949): 100–125.

Pargeter, Alison. "Libya: Reforming the Impossible?" *Review of African Political Economy* Vol. 33, No. 108, *North Africa: Power, Politics and Promise* (Jun. 2006): 219–235.

Rghei, Amer S. and J. G. Nelson. "The Conservation and Use of the Walled City of Tripoli." *Geographical Journal* Vol. 160, No. 2 (Jul. 1994): 143–158.

Rivlin, Benjamin. "Unity and Nationalism in Libya." *Middle East Journal* Vol. 3, No. 1 (Jan. 1949): 31–44.

Sammut, Dennis. "Libya and the Islamic Challenge." *World Today* Vol. 50, No. 10 (Oct. 1994): 198–200.

Sandford, K. S. "Western Frontiers of Libya Western Frontiers of Libya." *Geographical Journal* Vol. 99, No. 1 (Jan. 1942): 29–40.

Sandford, K. S. et al. "Problems of Modern Libya: Discussion." *Geographical Journal* Vol. 119, No. 2 (Jun. 1953): 195–199.

Sanger, Richard H. "Libya: Conclusions on an Unfinished Revolution." *Middle East Journal* Vol. 29, No. 4 (Autumn 1975): 409–417.

Schumacher, Edward. "The United States and Libya." *Foreign Affairs* Vol. 65, No. 2 (Winter 1986): 329–348.

Schwartz, Jonathan B. "Dealing with a 'Rogue State': The Libya Precedent." *American Journal of International Law* Vol. 101, No. 3 (Jul. 2007): 553–580.

Segal, Aaron. "Libya's Economic Potential." *World Today* Vol. 28, No. 10 (Oct. 1972): 445–451.

Segre, Claudio G. "Italo Balbo and the Colonization of Libya." *Journal of Contemporary History* Vol. 7, No. 3/4 (Jul.–Oct. 1972): 141–155.

Shaw, W. B. K. "International Boundaries of Libya." *Geographical Journal* Vol. 85, No. 1 (Jan. 1935): 50–53.

Solomon, Hussein and Gerrie Swart. "Libya's Foreign Policy in Flux." *African Affairs* Vol. 104, No. 416 (Jul. 2005): 469–492.

St. John, Ronald Bruce. "The Soviet Penetration of Libya." *The World Today* Vol. 38, No. 4 (Apr., 1982): 131–138.

St. John, Ronald Bruce. " 'Libya Is Not Iraq': Preemptive Strikes, W.M.D. and Diplomacy." *Middle East Journal* Vol. 58, No. 3 (Summer 2004): 386–402.

Takeyh, Ray. "The Rogue Who Came in from the Cold." *Foreign Affairs* Vol. 80, No. 3 (May–Jun. 2001): 62–72.

"U.S. Raid Haunts Libya." *MERIP Middle East Report* No. 141, *Hidden Wars* (Jul.–Aug., 1986): 35–37.

Vandewalle, Dirk. "Libya's Revolution Revisited." *MERIP Middle East Report* No. 143, *Nuclear Shadow over the Middle East* (Nov.–Dec., 1986): 30–35, 43.

Vandewalle, Dirk. "Qadhafi's 'Perestroika': Economic and Political Liberalization in Libya." *Middle East Journal* Vol. 45, No. 2 (Spring 1991): 216–231.

Von Henneberg, Krystyna. "Imperial Uncertainties: Architectural Syncretism and Improvisation in Fascist Colonial Libya." *Journal of Contemporary History* Vol. 31, No. 2, *Special Issue: The Aesthetics of Fascism* (Apr. 1996): 373–395.

Ward, Philip. "Contemporary Art in Libya." *African Arts* Vol. 4, No. 4 (Summer 1971): 40, 43–80.

Wright, Claudia. "Libya and the West: Headlong into Confrontation?" *International Affairs (Royal Institute of International Affairs 1944)* Vol. 58, No. 1 (Winter 1981–1982): 13–41.

Zoubir, Yahia H. "Libya in U.S. Foreign Policy: From Rogue State to Good Fellow?" *Third World Quarterly* Vol. 23, No. 1 (Feb. 2002): 31–53.

Index

About the Authors

TOYIN FALOLA is a University Distinguished Teaching Professor, University of Texas at Austin, and author of many books including *Culture and Customs of Nigeria*.

JASON MORGAN is a graduate student in the History Department at the University of Texas. He specializes in twentieth century African and international history.

BUKOLA ADEYEMI OYENIYI is a Research Fellow at the Institute for Advanced Study, New Europe College, Bucharest, Romania. He teaches history and international studies at the Joseph Ayo Babalola University, Nigeria.